MECHANICS 73

22.	Capitalization	74
23.	Abbreviations, numbers, and italics (underlining)	76
24.	Spelling and the hyphen	81

RESEARCHED WRITING 86

25.	Supporting a thesis	87
26.	When to cite a source; avoiding plagiarism	91
27.	How to integrate quotations	95
28.	How to integrate other source material	99

DOCUMENTATION 102

29.	MLA documentation style	103
30.	ACW style: Documenting Internet sources	122
31.	APA documentation style	123
32.	*Chicago* documentation style (footnotes or endnotes)	137
33.	A list of style manuals	156

GLOSSARIES 158

34.	Glossary of usage	159
35.	Glossary of grammatical terms	168

INDEX	176
CHECKLIST FOR GLOBAL REVISION	186
CORRECTION SYMBOLS	187

How to use this book

A Pocket Style Manual is a quick reference for writers and researchers. As a writer, you can turn to it for advice on revising sentences for clarity, grammar, punctuation, and mechanics. As a researcher, you can refer to its documentation models and to its guidelines on developing and supporting a thesis and citing and integrating sources. Three commonly used documentation styles are included: MLA, APA, and *Chicago*-style footnotes or endnotes.

Here are the book's reference features.

The brief or detailed contents. The brief table of contents inside the front cover will usually send you very close to the information you're looking for. Once you have turned to a particular section, you'll find that the book's many headings help you scan for the exact advice you need.

Occasionally you may want to consult the more detailed contents inside the back cover.

The index. If you aren't sure what topic to choose from one of the tables of contents, consult the index at the back of the book. For example, you may not realize that the choice between *is* and *are* is a matter of subject-verb agreement (10 in the brief contents). In that case, simply look up "*is* versus *are*" in the index and you will be directed to the pages you need.

Indexes to documentation models. Each style of documentation—MLA, APA, and *Chicago*—includes directories to its citation and bibliographic models. The MLA directories, for example, are on pages 103 and 108–09. The pages with MLA models are edged in red for easy reference. If your professor requires APA or *Chicago* style, you might flag these pages with paper clips.

The glossaries. When in doubt about the correct use of a particular word (such as *affect* and *effect, among* and *between,* or *hopefully*), consult section 34, a glossary of usage. When you don't understand the meaning of a grammatical term used elsewhere in the book, consult section 35, a glossary of grammatical terms. There you will find brief definitions of terms such as *adjective, adverb, subordinate clause,* and *participial phrase.*

A Pocket Style Manual is meant to be consulted as the need arises. Keep it on your desk—right next to your dictionary—or tuck it into your backpack or jacket pocket and carry it with you as a ready resource.

A POCKET STYLE MANUAL

Second Edition

Clarity

Grammar

Punctuation and Mechanics

Research

Documentation

Usage/Grammatical Terms

Diana Hacker

Bedford Books ≋ Boston

For Bedford Books

President and Publisher: Charles H. Christensen
General Manager and Associate Publisher: Joan E. Feinberg
Managing Editor: Elizabeth M. Schaaf
Developmental Editor: Beth Castrodale
Editorial Assistant: Joanne Diaz
Production Editor: Heidi L. Hood
Copyeditor: Barbara G. Flanagan
Text Design: Claire Seng-Niemoeller
Cover Design: Hannus Design Associates

Library of Congress Catalog Card Number: 96–86775

Manufactured in the United States of America.

1 0 9 8 7 6
f e d c b a

For information, write: Bedford Books, 75 Arlington Street,
Boston, MA 02116   (617-426-7440)

ISBN: 0–312–11596–2

Acknowledgment

Janice R. Walker, specifications from style sheet endorsed
by the Alliance for Computers and Writing. Copyright ©
J. Walker 1996. Reprinted by permission of the author.

CLARITY

Clarity

1. Tighten wordy sentences.

Long sentences are not necessarily wordy, nor are short sentences always concise. A sentence is wordy if its meaning can be gracefully conveyed in fewer words.

1a. Redundancies

Redundancies such as *cooperate together, close proximity, basic essentials,* and *true fact* are a common source of wordiness. There is no need to say the same thing twice.

▶ Slaves were ~~portrayed or~~ stereotyped as lazy even though they were the main labor force of the South.

▶ Daniel ~~is now employed~~ at a rehabilitation center *works* ~~working~~ as a physical therapist.

Modifiers are redundant when their meanings are suggested by other words in the sentence.

▶ Sylvia ~~very hurriedly~~ scribbled her name and phone number on the back of a greasy napkin.

1b. Empty or inflated phrases

An empty word or phrase can be cut with little or no loss of meaning. An inflated phrase can be reduced to a word or two.

▶ ~~The town of~~ New Harmony, ~~located in~~ Indiana, was founded as a utopian community.

▶ We will file the appropriate papers ~~in the event that~~ *if* we are unable to meet the deadline.

INFLATED	CONCISE
along the lines of	like
at the present time	now, currently
because of the fact that	because
by means of	by

INFLATED	CONCISE
due to the fact that	because
for the reason that	because
in order to	to
in spite of the fact that	although, though
in the event that	if
until such time as	until

1c. Needlessly complex structures

In a rough draft, sentence structures are often more complex than they need to be.

▶ ~~There is~~ *A*nother videotape ~~that~~ tells the story of

Charles Darwin and introduces the theory of

evolution.

▶ ~~It is imperative that~~ *A*ll police officers **must** follow strict

procedures when apprehending a suspect.

▶ The financial analyst claimed that because of volatile

market conditions she could not ~~make an~~ estimate

~~of~~ the company's future profits.

2. Prefer active verbs.

As a rule, active verbs express meaning more vigorously than their duller counterparts — forms of the verb *be* or verbs in the passive voice. Forms of *be* (*be, am, is, are, was, were, being,* and *been*) lack vigor because they convey no action. Passive verbs lack strength because their subjects receive the action instead of doing it.

Although forms of *be* and passive verbs have legitimate uses, if an active verb can convey your meaning as well, use it.

FORM OF *BE*	A surge of power *was* responsible for the destruction of the coolant pumps.
PASSIVE	The coolant pumps *were destroyed* by a surge of power.
ACTIVE	A surge of power *destroyed* the coolant pumps.

2a. When to replace *be* verbs

Not every *be* verb needs replacing. The forms of *be* (*be, am, is, are, was, were, being, been*) work well when you want to link a subject to a noun that clearly renames it or to a vivid adjective that describes it: *Advertising is legalized lying. Great intellects are skeptical.*

If a *be* verb makes a sentence needlessly wordy, however, consider replacing it. Often a phrase following the verb will contain a word (such as *destruction*) that suggests a more vigorous, active alternative (*destroyed*).

▶ Burying nuclear waste in Antarctica would ~~be in violation of~~ *violate* an international treaty.

▶ When Rosa Parks ~~was resistant to~~ *resisted* giving up her seat on the bus, she became a civil rights hero.

2b. When to replace passive verbs

In the active voice, the subject of the sentence does the action; in the passive, the subject receives the action.

ACTIVE   The committee reached a decision.

PASSIVE   A decision was reached by the committee.

In passive sentences, the actor (in this case *committee*) frequently disappears from the sentence: *A decision was reached.*

In most cases, you will want to emphasize the actor, so you should use the active voice. To replace a passive verb with an active alternative, make the actor the subject of the sentence.

▶ ~~The transformer was struck by a bolt of lightning,~~ *A bolt of lightning struck the transformer,* plunging us into darkness.

▶ As the patient undressed, scars ~~were seen~~ *the doctor saw* on her back, stomach, and thighs.

The passive voice is appropriate when you wish to emphasize the receiver of the action or to minimize the importance of the actor. In the following sentence, for example, the writer wished to focus on the tobacco plants, not on the people spraying them: *As the time for harvest approaches, the tobacco plants are sprayed with a chemical to retard the growth of suckers.*

3. Balance parallel ideas.

If two or more ideas are parallel, they should be expressed in parallel grammatical form.

> A kiss can be a comma, a question mark, or an exclamation point. — Mistinguett

> This novel is not to be tossed lightly aside, but to be hurled with great force. — Dorothy Parker

3a. Items in a series

Balance all items in a series by presenting them in parallel grammatical form.

▶ Abused children commonly exhibit one or more of the following symptoms: withdrawal, rebelliousness, restlessness, and ~~they are depressed~~.
   depression.

▶ The system has capabilities such as communicating with other computers, processing records, and *performing* mathematical functions.

▶ After assuring us that he was sober, Sam drove down the middle of the road, ran one red light, and *went through* two stop signs.

3b. Paired ideas

When pairing ideas, underscore their connection by expressing them in similar grammatical form. Paired ideas are usually connected in one of three ways: (1) with a coordinating conjunction such as *and, but,* or *or;* (2) with a pair of correlative conjunctions such as *either . . . or, not only . . . but also,* or *whether . . . or;* or (3) with a word introducing a comparison, usually *than* or *as.*

▶ Many states are reducing property taxes for home-
owners and ~~extend~~ *extending* financial aid in the form of tax
credits to renters.

The coordinating conjunction *and* connects two verbs: *reducing . . . extending.*

▶ The shutters were not only too long but also ~~were~~
too wide.

The correlative conjunctions *not only . . . but also* connect two adjective phrases: *too long . . . too wide.*

▶ It is easier to speak in abstractions than ~~grounding~~ *to ground*
one's thoughts in reality.

The comparative term *than* links two infinitive phrases: *to speak . . . to ground.*

4. Add needed words.

Do not omit words necessary for grammatical or logical completeness. Readers need to see at a glance how the parts of a sentence are connected.

4a. Words in compound structures

In compound structures, words are often omitted for economy: *Tom is a man who means what he says and* [*who*] *says what he means.* Such omissions are acceptable as long as the omitted word is common to both parts of the compound structure.

If the shorter version defies grammar or idiom because an omitted word is not common to both parts of the structure, the word must be put back in.

▶ Some of the regulars are acquaintances whom we
 who
 see at work or live in our community.
  ^

 The word *who* must be included because *whom live in our community* is not grammatically correct.

  accepted
▶ I never have and never will accept a bribe.
   ^

 Have . . . accept is not grammatically correct.

  in
▶ Tribes in the South Pacific still believe and live by
   ^

 ancient laws.

 Believe . . . by is not idiomatic English.

4b. The word *that*
Add the word *that* if there is any danger of misreading without it.

  that
▶ Many citizens do not believe the leaders of this
  ^

 administration are serious about reducing the deficit.

 Without *that,* readers might at first think that the citizens don't believe the leaders.

4c. Words in comparisons
Comparisons should be between items that are alike. To compare unlike items is illogical and distracting.

   those of
▶ Their starting salaries are higher than other
    ^

 professionals with more seniority.

 Salaries must be compared with salaries, not with professionals.

5. Eliminate confusing shifts.

5a. Shifts in point of view
The point of view of a piece of writing is the perspective from which it is written: first person (*I* or *we*), second person (*you*), or third person (*he/she/it/one* or *they*).

Writers who are having difficulty settling on an appropriate point of view sometimes shift confusingly from one to another. The solution is to choose a suitable perspective and then stay with it.

▶   One week our class met to practice rescuing a victim
     We   *our*
     trapped in a wrecked car. ~~You~~ were graded on ~~your~~
              our   ^
     speed and ~~your~~ skill.
              ^

▶   With a little self-discipline and a desire to improve
     yourself,
     ~~oneself,~~ you too can enjoy the benefits of running.
     ^

Shifts from the third-person singular to the third-person plural are especially common.

     Police officers are
▶   ~~A police officer is~~ often criticized for always being
              ^
     there when they aren't needed and never being

     there when they are.

Although the writer might have changed *they* to *he or she* (to match the singular *officer*), the revision in the plural is more concise. See pages 28–31.

NOTE: The *I* (or *we*) point of view, which emphasizes the writer, is a good choice for writing based primarily on personal experience. The *you* point of view, which emphasizes the reader, works well for giving advice or explaining how to do something. The third-person point of view, which emphasizes the subject, is appropriate in most academic and professional writing.

5b. Shifts in tense

Consistent verb tenses clearly establish the time of the actions being described. When a passage begins in one tense and then shifts without warning and for no reason to another, readers are distracted and confused.

▶   Rescue workers put water on her face and lifted her
                                   opened
     head gently onto a pillow. Finally, she ~~opens~~ her
                                             ^
     eyes.

Writers often shift verb tenses when writing about literature. The literary convention is to describe fictional events consistently in the present tense. (See p. 27.)

▶ The scarlet letter is a punishment sternly placed on

Hester's breast by the community, and yet it ~~was~~ an
    is

extremely fanciful and imaginative product of

Hester's own needlework.

6. Untangle mixed constructions.

A mixed construction contains parts that do not sensibly fit together. The mismatch may be a matter of grammar or of logic.

6a. Mixed grammar

A writer should not begin with one grammatical plan and then switch without warning to another.

▶ For ~~m~~ost drivers who have a blood alcohol content of
    M

.05 percent double their risk of causing an accident.

The phrase beginning with *For* cannot serve as the subject of the sentence. If the phrase opens the sentence, it must be followed by a subject and a verb: *For most drivers who have a blood alcohol content of .05 percent, the risk of causing an accident is doubled.*

▶ Although many pre-Columbian peoples achieved a

high level of civilization, ~~but~~ they were unfamiliar

with the wheel.

The *Although* clause is subordinate, so it cannot be linked to an independent clause with the coordinating conjunction *but.*

6b. Illogical connections

A sentence's subject and verb should make sense together.

▶ Under the revised plan, the elderly~~/who now receive a~~
the double personal exemption for

~~double personal exemption,~~ will be abolished.

The exemption, not the elderly, will be abolished.

Tiffany
▶ We decided that ~~Tiffany's welfare~~ would not be safe

living with her mother.

Tiffany, not her welfare, may not be safe.

7. Repair misplaced and dangling modifiers.

Modifiers should point clearly to the words they modify. As a rule, related words should be kept together.

7a. Misplaced words

The most commonly misplaced words are limiting modifiers such as *only, even, almost, nearly,* and *just.* They should appear in front of a verb only if they modify the verb: *At first I couldn't even touch my toes.* If they limit the meaning of some other word in the sentence, they should be placed in front of that word.

only
▶ Lasers ~~only~~ destroy the target, leaving the surrounding

healthy tissue intact.

7b. Misplaced phrases and clauses

Although phrases and clauses can appear at some distance from the words they modify, make sure your meaning is clear. When phrases or clauses are oddly placed, absurd misreadings can result.

On the walls
▶ ~~There~~ are many pictures of comedians who have

performed at Gavin's • ~~on the walls~~.

The comedians weren't performing on the walls; the pictures were on the walls.

▶ The robber was described as a six-foot-tall man *150-pound,* ^

with a mustache. ~~weighing 150 pounds.~~ ^

The robber, not the mustache, weighed 150 pounds.

7c. Dangling modifiers

A dangling modifier fails to refer logically to any word in the sentence. Dangling modifiers are usually introductory word groups that suggest but do not name an actor. When a sentence opens with such a modifier, readers expect the subject of the following clause to name the actor. If it doesn't, the modifier dangles.

DANGLING

Upon entering the doctor's office, a skeleton caught my attention.

This sentence suggests—absurdly—that the skeleton entered the doctor's office.

To repair a dangling modifier, you can revise the sentence in one of two ways:

1. Name the actor immediately following the introductory modifier, or
2. turn the modifier into a word group that names the actor.

▶ Upon entering the doctor's office, a skeleton. *I noticed* ~~caught~~ ^ ^

~~my attention.~~

▶ ~~Upon entering~~ *As I entered* the doctor's office, a skeleton caught ^

my attention.

A dangling modifier cannot be repaired simply by moving it: *A skeleton caught my attention upon entering the doctor's office.* The sentence still suggests that the skeleton entered the doctor's office.

▶ ~~Opening~~ *When the driver opened* the window to let out a huge bumblebee, ^

the car accidentally swerved into an oncoming car.

The car didn't open the window; the driver did. The writer has revised the sentence by mentioning the driver in the opening modifier.

▶ After completing seminary training, ~~women's~~ access

    women have often been denied

to the pulpit. ~~has often been denied.~~

The women (not their access to the pulpit) complete the training. The writer has revised the sentence by making *women* (not *women's access*) the subject.

7d. Split infinitives

An infinitive consists of *to* plus a verb: *to think, to dance.* When a modifier appears between its two parts, an infinitive is said to be "split": *to carefully balance.* If a split infinitive is awkward, move the modifier to another position in the sentence.

▶ The jurors were instructed to ~~very carefully~~ sift

    very carefully.

through the evidence⁄

When a split infinitive is more natural and less awkward than alternative phrasing, most readers find it acceptable. *We decided to actually enforce the law* is a perfectly natural construction in English. *We decided actually to enforce the law* is not.

8. Provide some variety.

When a rough draft is filled with too many same-sounding sentences, try to inject some variety — as long as you can do so without sacrificing clarity or ease of reading.

8a. Combining choppy sentences

If a series of short sentences sounds choppy, consider combining some of them. Look for opportunities to tuck some of your ideas into subordinate clauses. Subordinate clauses, which contain subjects and verbs, begin with words like these: *after, although, because, before, if, since, that, unless, until, when, where, which,* and *who.*

    who

▶ The losing team was made up of superstars⁄~~They~~

acted as isolated individuals on the court.

▶ We keep our use of insecticides, herbicides, and

    because we
fungicides to a minimum. ~~We~~ are concerned about
        ^

the environment.

Also look for opportunities to tuck some of your ideas into phrases, word groups that lack subjects or verbs (or both).

▶ The Chesapeake and Ohio Canal, ~~is~~ a 184-mile
        ^

    waterway constructed in the 1800s. ~~It~~ was a major
                    ^

    source of transportation for goods during the

    Civil War.

    Noticing   *James*
▶ ~~James noticed~~ that the sky was glowing orange. ~~He~~
  ^   ^

    bent down to crawl into the bunker.

At times it will make sense to combine short sentences by joining them with *and, but,* or *or.*

                                        and
▶ Shore houses were flooded up to the first floor. Brandt's
                                          ^

    Lighthouse was swallowed by the sea.

CAUTION: Avoid stringing a series of sentences together with *and, but,* or *or.* For sentence variety, place some of the ideas in subordinate clauses or phrases.

    After four hours,
▶ ~~Four hours went by, and~~ a rescue truck finally
  ^

    arrived, but by that time we had been evacuated in a

    helicopter.

▶ These particles, ~~are~~ known as "stealth liposomes,"
                ^

    ~~and they~~ can hide in the body for a long time

    without detection.

8b. Varying sentence openings

Most sentences in English begin with the subject, move to the verb, and continue to an object, with modifiers tucked in along the way or put at the end. For the most part, such sentences are fine. Put too many of them in a row, however, and they become monotonous.

Words, phrases, or clauses modifying the verb can often be inserted ahead of the subject.

▶ *Eventually a*
A few drops of sap ~~eventually~~ began to trickle into
the pail.

▶ *Just as the sun was coming up, a*
A pair of black ducks flew over the pond. ~~just as the~~
~~sun was coming up.~~

Adjectives and participial phrases can frequently be moved to the beginning of a sentence without loss of clarity.

▶ *Dejected and withdrawn,*
Edward/ ~~dejected and withdrawn,~~ nearly gave up his
search for a job.

▶ *A* *John and I*
~~John and I,~~ anticipating a peaceful evening, sat down
at the campfire to brew a cup of coffee.

9. Find an appropriate voice.

An appropriate voice is one that suits your subject, engages your audience, and conforms to the conventions of the genre in which you are writing. When in doubt about the conventions of a particular genre — lab reports, informal essays, research papers, business memos, and so on — take a look at models written by experts in the field.

In the academic, professional, and business worlds, three kinds of language are generally considered inappropriate: jargon, which sounds too pretentious; slang, which sounds too casual; and sexist English, which offends many readers.

9a. Jargon

Jargon is specialized language used among members of a trade, profession, or group. Use jargon only when readers will be familiar with it; even then, use it only when plain English will not do as well.

JARGON   For many decades the majority body politic of South Africa attempted to negotiate legal enfranchisement without result.

REVISED   For many decades the majority population of South Africa negotiated in vain for the right to vote.

Broadly defined, jargon includes puffed-up language designed more to impress readers than to inform them. Common examples in business, government, higher education, and the military are given in the following list, with plain English translations in parentheses.

commence (begin)
components (parts)
endeavor (try)
exit (leave)
facilitate (help)
factor (consideration, cause)
finalize (finish)
impact on (affect)

indicator (sign)
input (advice)
optimal (best)
parameters (boundaries)
prior to (before)
prioritize (set priorities)
utilize (use)
viable (workable)

Sentences filled with jargon are hard to read, and they are often wordy as well.

▶   If managers ~~have adequate input from~~ *listen to* their subordinates, they can ~~effectuate more viable~~ *make better* decisions.

▶   All ~~employees functioning in the capacity of~~ work-study students ~~are required to give evidence of current enrollment.~~ *must prove that they are currently enrolled.*

9b. Slang

Slang is an informal and sometimes private vocabulary that expresses the solidarity of a group such as teenagers, rock musicians, or baseball fans. Although it does have a certain vitality, slang is a code that not everyone understands, and it is too informal for most written work.

▶   The government's "filth" guidelines will ~~gross you out.~~ *disgust you.*

▶   Mr. Hunnicutt's clothes were always ~~stylin'.~~ *fashionable.*

9c. Sexist language

Sexist language is language that stereotypes or demeans men or women, usually women. Such language arises from stereotypical thinking, from traditional pronoun use, and from words used to refer indefinitely to both sexes.

Stereotypical thinking.   In your writing, avoid referring to any one profession as exclusively male or exclusively female (such as referring to nurses in general as female). Also avoid using different conventions when identifying women and men (such as giving a woman's marital status but not a man's).

▶   All executives' ~~wives~~ *spouses* are invited to the picnic.

▶   Jake Stein, attorney, and ~~Mrs.~~ Cynthia Jones, ~~mother~~ *graphic designer,*

   ~~of three,~~ are running for city council.

The pronouns **he** ***and*** **him.**   Traditionally, *he, him,* and *his* were used to refer indefinitely to persons of either sex: *A journalist is stimulated by his deadline.* You can avoid such usage in one of three ways: substitute a pair of pronouns (*he or she, his or her*); reword in the plural; or revise the sentence to avoid the problem.

▶   A journalist is stimulated by his *or her* deadline.

▶   ~~A journalist is~~ *Journalists are* stimulated by ~~his deadline~~ *their deadlines.*

▶   A journalist is stimulated by ~~his~~ *a* deadline.

Man *words*.   Like *he* and *his,* the nouns *man* and *men* and related words containing them were once used indefinitely to refer to persons of either sex. Use gender-neutral terms instead.

INAPPROPRIATE	APPROPRIATE
chairman	chairperson, chair
congressman	representative, legislator
fireman	firefighter
mailman	mail carrier, postal worker
mankind	people, humans
to man	to operate, to staff
weatherman	meteorologist, forecaster
workman	worker, laborer

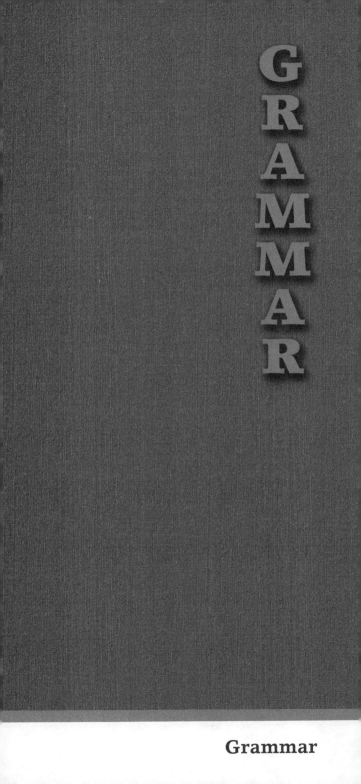

Grammar

10. Make subjects and verbs agree.

In the present tense, verbs agree with their subjects in number (singular or plural) and in person (first, second, or third). The present-tense ending -s is used on a verb if its subject is third-person singular; otherwise the verb takes no ending. Consider, for example, the present-tense forms of the verb *give*:

	SINGULAR	**PLURAL**
FIRST PERSON	I give	we give
SECOND PERSON	you give	you give
THIRD PERSON	he/she/it gives	they give
	Alison gives	parents give

The verb *be* varies from this pattern, and unlike any other verb it has special forms in *both* the present and the past tense.

PRESENT-TENSE FORMS OF BE		**PAST-TENSE FORMS OF BE**	
I am	we are	I was	we were
you are	you are	you were	you were
he/she/it is	they are	he/she/it was	they were

Problems with subject-verb agreement tend to arise in certain tricky contexts, which are detailed in this section.

10a. Words between subject and verb

Word groups often come between the subject and the verb. Such word groups, usually modifying the subject, may contain a noun that at first appears to be the subject. By mentally stripping away such modifiers, you can isolate the noun that is in fact the subject.

The *tulips* in the pot on the balcony *need* watering.

▶ High levels of air pollution damages the

respiratory tract.

The subject is *levels*, not *pollution*.

▶ The slaughter of pandas for their pelts ~~have~~
   has
   caused the panda population to decline drastically.

The subject is *slaughter*, not *pandas* or *pelts*.

NOTE: Phrases beginning with the prepositions *as well as, in addition to, accompanied by, together with,* and *along with* do not make a singular subject plural: *My sister, accompanied by her husband, was* [not *were*] *seated at the head table.*

10b. Subjects joined by *and*

Compound subjects joined by *and* are nearly always plural.

▶ Jill's natural ability and her desire to help others
   have
   ~~has~~ led to a career in the ministry.

EXCEPTION: If the parts of the subject form a single unit, however, you may treat the subject as singular: *Bacon and eggs is my favorite breakfast.*

10c. Subjects joined by *or* or *nor*

With compound subjects connected by *or* or *nor*, make the verb agree with the part of the subject nearer to the verb.

▶ If a relative or neighbor ~~are~~ abusing a child,
   is
   notify the police.

▶ Neither the professor nor his assistants ~~was~~ able
   were
   to solve the mystery of the eerie glow in the
   laboratory.

10d. Indefinite pronouns such as *someone*

Indefinite pronouns refer to nonspecific persons or things. Even though the following indefinite pronouns may seem to have plural meanings, treat them as singular in formal English: *anybody, anyone, each, either, everybody, everyone, everything, neither, none, no one, somebody, someone, something.*

favors
▶ Nearly everyone on the panel ~~favor~~ the arms
control agreement.

has
▶ Each of the furrows ~~have~~ been seeded.

A few indefinite pronouns (*all, any, some*) may be singular or plural depending on the noun or pronoun they refer to: *Some of the lemonade has disappeared. Some of the rocks were slippery.*

10e. Collective nouns such as *jury*

Collective nouns such as *jury, committee, club, audience, crowd, class, troop, family,* and *couple* name a class or a group. In American English collective nouns are usually treated as singular: They emphasize the group as a unit.

meets
▶ The scout troop ~~meet~~ in our basement on Mondays.

Occasionally, when there is some reason to draw attention to the individual members of the group, a collective noun may be treated as plural: *A young couple were arguing about politics while holding hands.* (Only individuals can argue and hold hands.)

NOTE: When units of measurement are used collectively, treat them as singular: *Three-fourths of the pie has been eaten.* When they refer to individual persons or things, treat them as plural: *One-fourth of the children were sick.*

10f. Subject after verb

Verbs ordinarily follow subjects. When this normal order is reversed, it is easy to become confused.

are
▶ Of particular concern ~~is~~ penicillin and tetracycline,
antibiotics used to make animals more resistant
to disease.

The subject *penicillin and tetracycline* is plural.

The subject always follows the verb in sentences beginning with *there is* or *there are* (or *there was* or *there were*).

▶ There ~~was~~ a social worker and a crew of twenty

   were

volunteers.

The subject *worker and crew* is plural.

10g. *Who, which,* and *that*

Like most pronouns, the relative pronouns *who, which,* and *that* have antecedents, nouns or pronouns to which they refer. Relative pronouns used as subjects take verbs that agree with their antecedents.

Take a suit that travels well.

Problems arise with the constructions *one of the* and *only one of the*. As a rule, treat *one of the* constructions as plural, *only one of the* constructions as singular.

▶ Our ability to use language is one of the things

   set

that ~~sets~~ us apart from animals.

The antecedent of *that* is *things*, not *one*. Several things set us apart from animals.

▶ SEACON is the only one of our war games that

   emphasizes

~~emphasize~~ scientific and technical issues.

The antecedent of *that* is *one*, not *games*. Only one game emphasizes scientific and technical issues.

10h. Plural form, singular meaning

Words such as *athletics, economics, mathematics, physics, statistics, measles,* and *news* are usually singular, despite their plural form.

   is

▶ Statistics ~~are~~ among the most difficult courses in

our program.

EXCEPTION: When they describe separate items rather than a collective body of knowledge, words such as *ath-*

letics, mathematics, and *statistics* are plural: *The statistics on school retention rates are impressive.*

10i. Titles and words mentioned as words
Titles and words mentioned as words are singular.

▶ *Lost Cities* ~~describe~~ **describes** the discoveries of many ancient civilizations.

▶ *Controlled substances* ~~are~~ **is** a euphemism for illegal drugs.

11. Be alert to other problems with verbs.

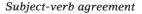

The verb is the heart of the sentence, so it is important to get it right. Section 10 deals with the problem of subject-verb agreement. This section describes a few other potential problems with verbs.

11a. Irregular verbs
For all regular verbs, the past-tense and past-participle forms are the same, ending in *-ed* or *-d,* so there is no danger of confusion. This is not true, however, for irregular verbs such as the following.

BASE FORM	PAST TENSE	PAST PARTICIPLE
begin	began	begun
fly	flew	flown
ride	rode	ridden

The past-tense form, which never has a helping verb, expresses action that occurred entirely in the past. The past participle is used with a helping verb — either with *has, have,* or *had* to form one of the perfect tenses or with *be, am, is, are, was, were, being,* or *been* to form the passive voice.

PAST TENSE	Last July, we *went* to Paris.
PAST PARTICIPLE	We have *gone* to Paris twice.

When you aren't sure which verb form to choose (*went* or *gone*, *began* or *begun*, and so on), consult the list that begins on page 24. Choose the past-tense form if your sentence doesn't have a helping verb; choose the past-participle form if it does.

▶ Yesterday we ~~seen~~ an unidentified flying object.
    saw

Because there is no helping verb, the past-tense form *saw* is required.

▶ The driver had apparently ~~fell~~ asleep at the wheel.
         fallen

Because of the helping verb *had*, the past-participle form *fallen* is required.

***Distinguishing between* lie *and* lay.** Writers often confuse the forms of *lie* (meaning "to recline or rest on a surface") and *lay* (meaning "to put or place something"). The intransitive verb *lie* does not take a direct object: *The tax forms are lying on the coffee table.* The transitive verb *lay* takes a direct object: *Please lay the tax forms on the coffee table.*

In addition to confusing the meanings of *lie* and *lay*, writers are often unfamiliar with the standard English forms of these verbs. Their past-tense and past-participle forms are given in the list of common irregular verbs that begins on page 24. The present participle of *lie* is *lying*; the present participle of *lay* is *laying*.

▶ Elizabeth was so exhausted that she ~~laid~~ down
               lay

for a nap.

The past-tense form of *lie* ("to recline") is *lay*.

▶ Mary ~~lay~~ the baby on my lap.
  laid

The past-tense form of *lay* ("to place") is *laid*.

▶ My mother's letters were ~~laying~~ in the corner of the
          lying

chest.

The present participle of *lie* ("to rest on a surface") is *lying*.

Common irregular verbs

BASE FORM	PAST TENSE	PAST PARTICIPLE
arise	arose	arisen
awake	awoke, awaked	awaked, awoke
be	was, were	been
beat	beat	beaten, beat
become	became	become
begin	began	begun
bend	bent	bent
bite	bit	bitten, bit
blow	blew	blown
break	broke	broken
bring	brought	brought
build	built	built
burst	burst	burst
buy	bought	bought
catch	caught	caught
choose	chose	chosen
cling	clung	clung
come	came	come
cost	cost	cost
deal	dealt	dealt
dig	dug	dug
dive	dived, dove	dived
do	did	done
drag	dragged	dragged
draw	drew	drawn
dream	dreamed, dreamt	dreamed, dreamt
drink	drank	drunk
drive	drove	driven
eat	ate	eaten
fall	fell	fallen
fight	fought	fought
find	found	found
fly	flew	flown
forget	forgot	forgotten, forgot
freeze	froze	frozen
get	got	gotten, got
give	gave	given
go	went	gone
grow	grew	grown
hang (suspend)	hung	hung
hang (execute)	hanged	hanged
have	had	had
hear	heard	heard
hide	hid	hidden
hurt	hurt	hurt
keep	kept	kept
know	knew	known

BASE FORM	PAST TENSE	PAST PARTICIPLE
lay (put)	laid	laid
lead	led	led
lend	lent	lent
let (allow)	let	let
lie (recline)	lay	lain
lose	lost	lost
make	made	made
prove	proved	proved, proven
read	read	read
ride	rode	ridden
ring	rang	rung
rise (get up)	rose	risen
run	ran	run
say	said	said
see	saw	seen
send	sent	sent
set (place)	set	set
shake	shook	shaken
shoot	shot	shot
shrink	shrank	shrunk, shrunken
sing	sang	sung
sink	sank	sunk
sit (be seated)	sat	sat
slay	slew	slain
sleep	slept	slept
speak	spoke	spoken
spin	spun	spun
spring	sprang	sprung
stand	stood	stood
steal	stole	stolen
sting	stung	stung
strike	struck	struck, stricken
swear	swore	sworn
swim	swam	swum
swing	swung	swung
take	took	taken
teach	taught	taught
throw	threw	thrown
wake	woke, waked	waked, woken
wear	wore	worn
wring	wrung	wrung
write	wrote	written

11b. Tense

Tenses indicate the time of an action in relation to the time of the speaking or writing about that action. The most common problem with tenses — shifting from one tense to another — is discussed on pages 8–9. Other

problems with tenses are detailed in this section, after
the following survey of tenses.

Survey of tenses. Tenses are classified as present,
past, and future, with simple, perfect, and progressive
forms for each.

The simple tenses indicate relatively simple time
relations. The present tense is used primarily for actions occurring at the time of the speaking or for
actions occurring regularly. The past tense is used
for actions completed in the past. The future tense is
used for actions that will occur in the future. In the following table, the simple tenses are given for the regular verb *walk*, the irregular verb *ride*, and the highly
irregular verb *be*.

PRESENT TENSE

SINGULAR		PLURAL	
I	walk, ride, am	we	walk, ride, are
you	walk, ride, are	you	walk, ride, are
he/she/it	walks, rides, is	they	walk, ride, are

PAST TENSE

SINGULAR		PLURAL	
I	walked, rode, was	we	walked, rode, were
you	walked, rode, were	you	walked, rode, were
he/she/it	walked, rode, was	they	walked, rode, were

FUTURE TENSE

I, you, he/she/it, we, they	will walk, ride, be

More complex time relations are indicated by the
perfect tenses. A verb in one of the perfect tenses (a
form of *have* plus the past participle) expresses an action that was or will be completed at the time of another action.

PRESENT PERFECT

I, you, we, they	have walked, ridden, been
he/she/it	has walked, ridden, been

PAST PERFECT

I, you, he/she/it, we, they	had walked, ridden, been

FUTURE PERFECT

I, you, he/she/it, we, they	will have walked, ridden, been

Each of the six tenses just mentioned has a progressive form used to express a continuing action. A

progressive verb consists of a form of *be* followed by the present participle.

PRESENT PROGRESSIVE

I	am walking, riding, being
he/she/it	is walking, riding, being
you, we, they	are walking, riding, being

PAST PROGRESSIVE

I, he/she/it	was walking, riding, being
you, we, they	were walking, riding, being

FUTURE PROGRESSIVE

I, you, he/she/it, we, they	will be walking, riding, being

PRESENT PERFECT PROGRESSIVE

I, you, we, they	have been walking, riding, being
he/she/it	has been walking, riding, being

PAST PERFECT PROGRESSIVE

I, you, he/she/it, we, they	had been walking, riding, being

FUTURE PERFECT PROGRESSIVE

I, you, he/she/it, we, they	will have been walking, riding, being

Special uses of the present tense. Use the present tense when writing about literature or when expressing general truths.

▶ Don Quixote, in Cervantes's novel, ~~was~~ *is* an idealist

ill suited for life in the real world.

▶ Galileo taught that the earth ~~orbited~~ *orbits* the sun.

The past perfect tense. The past perfect tense is used for an action already completed by the time of another past action. This tense consists of a past participle preceded by *had* (*had worked, had gone*).

▶ We built our cabin forty feet above an abandoned

quarry that ~~was~~ *had been* flooded in 1920 to create a lake.

▶ In 1941 Hitler decided to kill the Jews. But

Himmler and his SS were three years ahead of

him; they *had* had mass murder in mind since 1938.

11c. Mood

There are three moods in English: the *indicative*, used for facts, opinions, and questions; the *imperative*, used for orders or advice; and the *subjunctive*, used for wishes, conditions contrary to fact, and requests or recommendations. Of these three moods, the subjunctive is most likely to cause problems.

Use the subjunctive mood for wishes and in *if* clauses expressing conditions contrary to fact. The subjunctive in such cases is the past tense form of the verb; in the case of *be*, it is always *were* (not *was*), even if the subject is singular.

> We asked that Janet *drive* more slowly.

> If I *were* a member of Congress, I would vote for the bill.

Use the subjunctive mood in *that* clauses following verbs such as *ask, insist, recommend,* and *request.* The subjunctive in such cases is the base (or dictionary) form of the verb.

> Dr. Chung insists that her students *be* on time.

> We recommend that Dawson *file* form 1050 soon.

11d. Voice

Transitive verbs (those that can take direct objects) appear in either the active or the passive voice. In the active voice, the subject of the sentence does the action; in the passive, the subject receives the action.

ACTIVE   John *hit* the ball.

PASSIVE   The ball *was hit* by John.

Because the active voice is simpler and more direct, it is usually more appropriate than the passive. (See section 2.)

12. Use pronouns with care.

Pronouns are words that substitute for nouns: *he, it, them, her, me,* and so on. Four frequently encountered problems with pronouns are discussed in this section:

a. pronoun-antecedent agreement (singular vs. plural)
b. pronoun reference (clarity)
c. case of personal pronouns (*I* vs. *me,* etc.)
d. *who* vs. *whom*

12a. Pronoun-antecedent agreement

The antecedent of a pronoun is the word the pronoun refers to. A pronoun and its antecedent agree when they are both singular or both plural.

SINGULAR   The *doctor* finished *her* rounds.

PLURAL   The *doctors* finished *their* rounds.

Writers are sometimes tempted to choose the plural pronoun *they* (or *their*) to refer to a singular antecedent. The temptation is greatest when the singular antecedent is an indefinite pronoun, a generic noun, or a collective noun.

Indefinite pronouns.   Indefinite pronouns refer to nonspecific persons or things. Even though some of the following indefinite pronouns may seem to have plural meanings, treat them as singular in formal English: *anybody, anyone, each, either, everybody, everyone, everything, neither, none, no one, someone, something.*

In this class *everyone* performs at *his or her* [not *their*] fitness level.

When *they* or *their* refers mistakenly to a singular antecedent such as *everyone,* you will usually have three options for revision:

1. Replace *they* with *he or she* (or *their* with *his or her*);
2. make the singular antecedent plural; or
3. rewrite the sentence.

Because the *he or she* construction is wordy, often the second or third revision strategy is more effective.

he or she is
▶ When someone has been drinking, ~~they are~~ more

   likely to speed.

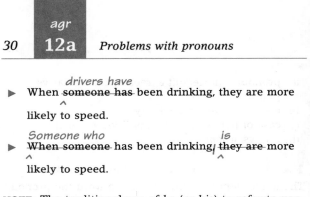

> *drivers have*
> When ~~someone has~~ been drinking, they are more
> ^
> likely to speed.

> *Someone who*   *is*
> When ~~someone~~ has been drinking, ~~they are~~ more
> ^   ^
> likely to speed.

NOTE: The traditional use of *he* (or *his*) to refer to persons of either sex is now widely considered sexist. (See p. 16.)

Generic nouns. A generic noun represents a typical member of a group, such as a student, or any member of a group, such as any musician. Although generic nouns may seem to have plural meanings, they are singular.

Every *runner* must train rigorously if *he or she* wants [not *they want*] to excel.

When *they* or *their* refers mistakenly to a generic noun, you will usually have the same three revision options as for indefinite pronouns.

> *he or she wants*
> A medical student must study hard if ~~they want~~ to
> ^
> succeed.

> *Medical students*
> ~~A medical student~~ must study hard if they want to
> ^
> succeed.

> A medical student must study hard ~~if they want~~ to
> succeed.

Collective nouns. Collective nouns such as *jury, committee, audience, crowd, family,* and *team* name a class or group. In American English, collective nouns are usually singular because they emphasize the group functioning as a unit.

The planning *committee* granted *its* [not *their*] permission to build.

If the members of the group function individually,
however, you may treat the noun as plural: *The family
put their signatures on the document.* Or you might add
a plural antecedent such as *members* to the sentence:
*The members of the family put their signatures on the
document.*

12b. Pronoun reference

A pronoun should refer clearly to its antecedent. A pronoun's reference will be unclear if it is ambiguous, implied, vague, or indefinite.

Ambiguous reference. Ambiguous reference occurs
when the pronoun could refer to two possible antecedents.

▶ When Aunt Harriet put ~~the cake~~ on the table, it
   it   *the cake*
   collapses.

▶ Tom told James, ~~that he had~~ won the lottery.
                  "You have   *"*

What collapsed — the cake or the table? Who won the
lottery — Tom or James? The revisions eliminate the
ambiguity.

Implied reference. A pronoun must refer to a specific antecedent, not to a word that is implied but not
present in the sentence.

▶ After braiding Ann's hair, Sue decorated ~~them~~ with
                                            the braids
   ribbons.

Modifiers, such as possessives, cannot serve as antecedents. A modifier merely implies the noun that the
pronoun might logically refer to.

▶ In ~~Euripides'~~ *Medea,* he describes the plight of a
      Euripides
   woman rejected by her husband.

***Vague reference of* this, that, *or* which.** The pro-
nouns *this, that,* and *which* should not refer vaguely to
earlier word groups or ideas. These pronouns should

refer to specific antecedents. When a pronoun's reference is too vague, either replace the pronoun with a noun or supply an antecedent to which the pronoun clearly refers.

▶   More and more often, especially in large cities, **we**

are finding ourselves victims of serious crimes. **We**
                                our fate
learn to accept ~~this~~ with minor complaints.
                       ^

▶   Romeo and Juliet were both too young to have
                              a fact
acquired much wisdom, which accounts for
                               ^

their rash actions.

Indefinite reference of *they, it, or you.*   The pronoun *they* should refer to a specific antecedent. Do not use *they* to refer indefinitely to persons who have not been specifically mentioned.

▶   Sometimes a list of ways to save energy is
                           the gas company suggests
included in the gas bill. For example, ~~they suggest~~
                                        ^
setting a moderate temperature for the hot water

heater.

The word *it* should not be used indefinitely in constructions such as "In the article it says that . . ."

     The
▶   ~~In the~~ encyclopedia ~~it~~ states that male moths can
    ^
smell female moths from several miles away.

The pronoun *you* is appropriate when the writer is addressing the reader directly: *Once you have kneaded the dough, let it rise in a warm place.* Except in informal contexts, however, the indefinite *you* (meaning "anyone in general") is inappropriate.

                        students
▶   In advanced chemistry ~~you~~ must work hard to
                           ^
earn a C.

12c. Case of personal pronouns (*I* versus *me*, etc.)

The personal pronouns in the following list change what is known as case form according to their grammatical function in a sentence. Pronouns functioning as subjects or subject complements appear in the *subjective* case; those functioning as objects appear in the *objective* case; and those functioning as possessives appear in the *possessive* case.

SUBJECTIVE CASE	OBJECTIVE CASE	POSSESSIVE CASE
I	me	my
we	us	our
you	you	your
he/she/it	him/her/it	his/her/its
they	them	their

For the most part, you know how to use these forms correctly. In the following situations, however, you may have difficulty choosing between *I* and *me*, *she* and *her*, and so on.

Compound word groups. When a subject or object appears as part of a compound structure, you may occasionally become confused. To test for the correct pronoun, mentally strip away all of the compound structure except the pronoun in question.

▶ While diving for pearls, Ikiko and ~~her~~ *she* found a

treasure chest full of gold bars.

> *Ikiko and she* is the subject of the verb *found*. Strip away the words *Ikiko and* to test for the correct pronoun: *she found* [not *her found*].

▶ The most traumatic experience for her father and ~~I~~ *me* occurred long after her operation.

> *Her father and me* is the object of the preposition *for*. Strip away the words *her father and* to test for the correct pronoun: *for me* [not *for I*].

Subject complements. Use subjective-case pronouns for subject complements, which rename or describe the subject and usually follow *be, am, is, are, was, were, being,* or *been.*

▶ During the Lindbergh trial, Bruno Hauptmann

                           he.

  repeatedly denied that the kidnapper was ~~him~~.

    If *kidnapper was he* seems too stilted, rewrite the sentence: *During the Lindbergh trial, Bruno Hauptmann repeatedly denied that he was the kidnapper.*

Appositives.   Appositives, noun phrases that rename nouns or pronouns, have the same function as the words they rename. To test for the correct pronoun, mentally strip away the words that the appositive renames.

                       I,

▶ The chief strategists, Dr. Bell and ~~me~~, could not

  agree on a plan.

    The appositive *Dr. Bell and I* renames the subject, *strategists.* Test: *I could not agree* [not *me could not agree*].

▶ The reporter interviewed only two witnesses, the

                  me.

  shopkeeper and ~~I~~.

    The appositive *the shopkeeper and me* renames the direct object, *witnesses.* Test: *interviewed me* [not *interviewed I*].

We *or* us *before a noun.*   When deciding whether *we* or *us* should precede a noun, choose the pronoun that would be appropriate if the noun were omitted.

   We

▶ ~~Us~~ tenants would rather fight than move.

    Test: *We would rather fight* [not *Us would rather fight*].

                        us

▶ Management is short-changing ~~we~~ tenants.

    Test: *Management is short-changing us* [not *Management is short-changing we*].

Pronoun after* than *or* as.   Sentence parts, usually verbs, are often omitted in comparisons beginning with *than* or *as.* To test for the correct pronoun, finish the sentence.

▶ My husband is six years older than ~~me~~. *I.*

Test: *than* I [*am*].

▶ We respected no other candidate in the election as
much as ~~she~~. *her.*

Test: *as* [*we respected*] *her*.

Pronoun before or after an infinitive.   An infinitive
is the word *to* followed by a verb. Both subjects and objects of infinitives take the objective case.

▶ Ms. Wilson asked John and ~~I~~ to drive the senator *me*
and ~~she~~ to the airport. *her*

John and me is the subject and *senator and her* is the
object of the infinitive *to drive*.

Pronoun or noun before a gerund.   If a pronoun
modifies a gerund, use the possessive case: *my, our,
your, his/her/its, their*. A gerund is a verb form ending
in *-ing* that functions as a noun.

▶ My parents always tolerated ~~us~~ talking after the *our*

lights were out.

Nouns as well as pronouns may modify gerunds. To
form the possessive case of a noun, use an apostrophe
and an *-s* (*a victim's suffering*) or just an apostrophe
(*victims' suffering*). (See pp. 63–64.)

▶ The old order in France paid a high price for the
~~aristocracy~~ exploiting the lower classes. *aristocracy's*

12d. *Who* or *whom*

Who, a subjective-case pronoun, can be used only for
subjects and subject complements. *Whom*, an objective-
case pronoun, can be used only for objects. The words
who and *whom* appear primarily in subordinate clauses
or in questions.

In subordinate clauses. When deciding whether to use *who* or *whom* in a subordinate clause, check for the word's function *within the clause*.

▶ He tells that story to ~~whomever~~ will listen.
    whoever

> *Whoever* is the subject of *will listen*. The entire subordinate clause *whoever will listen* is the object of the preposition *to*.

▶ You will work with our senior engineers, ~~who~~ you
    whom

will meet later.

> *Whom* is the direct object of the verb *will meet*. This becomes clear if you restructure the clause: *you will meet whom later*.

In questions. When deciding whether to use *who* or *whom* in a question, check for the word's function *within the question*.

▶ ~~Whom~~ was accused of receiving money from
    Who

the Mafia?

> *Who* is the subject of the verb *was accused*.

▶ ~~Who~~ did the Democratic Party nominate in 1976?
    Whom

> *Whom* is the direct object of the verb *did nominate*. This becomes clear if you restructure the question: *The Democratic Party did nominate whom in 1976?*

13. Choose adjectives and adverbs with care.

Adjectives modify nouns or pronouns; adverbs modify verbs, adjectives, or other adverbs.

Many adverbs are formed by adding -*ly* to adjectives (*formal, formally*). But don't assume that all words ending in -*ly* are adverbs or that all adverbs end in -*ly*. Some adjectives end in -*ly* (*lovely, friendly*) and some adverbs don't (*always*, *here*). When in doubt, consult a dictionary.

13a. Adverbs

Use adverbs, not adjectives, to modify verbs, adjectives, and adverbs. Adverbs usually answer one of these questions: When? Where? How? Why? Under what conditions? How often? To what degree?

The incorrect use of adjectives in place of adverbs to modify verbs occurs primarily in casual or nonstandard speech.

perfectly
▶ The arrangement worked out ~~perfect~~ for everyone.
                              ^

The incorrect use of the adjective *good* in place of the adverb *well* is especially common in casual and nonstandard speech.

well
▶ We were delighted that Nicole had done so ~~good~~
                                             ^
  on the exam.

Adjectives are sometimes incorrectly used to modify adjectives or other adverbs.

▶ In the early 1970s, chances for survival of the bald
really
  eagle looked ~~real~~ slim.
               ^

13b. Adjectives

Adjectives ordinarily precede nouns, but they can also function as subject complements following linking verbs (usually a form of *be*: *be, am, is, are, was, were, being, been*). When an adjective functions as a subject complement, it describes the subject.

Justice is *blind*.

Problems can arise with verbs such as *smell, taste, look, appear, grow,* and *feel,* which may or may not be linking. If the word following one of these verbs describes the subject, use an adjective; if it modifies the verb, use an adverb.

ADJECTIVE   The detective looked *cautious*.

ADVERB   The detective looked *cautiously* for the fingerprints.

Linking verbs usually suggest states of being, not actions. For example, to look cautious suggests the state of being cautious, whereas to look cautiously is to perform an action in a cautious way.

► Some flowers smell surprisingly ~~badly.~~ *bad.*

► Lori looked ~~well~~ in her new raincoat. *good*

The verbs *smell* and *looked* suggest states of being, not actions, so they should be followed by adjectives.

13c. Comparatives and superlatives

Most adjectives and adverbs have three forms: the positive, the comparative, and the superlative.

POSITIVE	COMPARATIVE	SUPERLATIVE
soft	softer	softest
fast	faster	fastest
careful	more careful	most careful
bad	worse	worst
good	better	best

Comparative versus superlative.   Use the comparative to compare two things, the superlative to compare three or more.

► Which of these two brands of toothpaste is ~~best?~~ *better?*

► Hobbs is the ~~more~~ qualified of the three applicants. *most*

Form of comparatives and superlatives.   To form comparatives and superlatives of most one- and two-syllable adjectives, use the endings *-er* and *-est: smooth, smoother, smoothest*. With longer adjectives, use *more* and *most* (or *less* and *least*): *exciting, more exciting, most exciting*.

Some one-syllable adverbs take the endings *-er* and *-est* (*fast, faster, fastest*), but longer adverbs and all of those ending in *-ly* use *more* and *most* (or *less* and *least*).

14. Repair sentence fragments.

As a rule, do not treat a piece of a sentence as if it were a sentence. To be a sentence, a word group must consist of at least one full independent clause. An independent clause has a subject and a verb, and it either stands alone as a sentence or could stand alone. Some fragments are clauses that contain a subject and a verb but begin with a subordinating word. Others are phrases that lack a subject, a verb, or both.

You can repair a fragment in one of two ways: Either pull the fragment into a nearby sentence, punctuating the new sentence correctly, or turn the fragment into a sentence.

14a. Fragmented clauses

A subordinate clause is patterned like a sentence, with both a subject and a verb, but it begins with a word that tells readers it cannot stand alone — a word such as *after, although, because, before, if, so that, that, though, unless, until, when, where, who,* and *which.*

Most fragmented clauses beg to be pulled into a sentence nearby.

▶ Jane will address the problem of limited on-campus
   if
   parking. If she is elected special student adviser.

If a fragmented clause cannot be gracefully combined with a nearby sentence, try rewriting it. The simplest way to turn a fragmented clause into a sentence is to delete the opening word or words that mark it as subordinate.

▶ Violence has produced much fear among teachers
                                    S
   at Dean Junior High. So that self-preservation, in
   fact, has become their primary aim.

14b. Fragmented phrases

Like subordinate clauses, certain phrases are sometimes mistaken for sentences. Frequently a fragmented phrase may simply be attached to a nearby sentence.

▶ The archaeologists worked slowly/, ~~E~~xamining and

labeling every pottery shard they uncovered.

The word group beginning with *Examining* is a verbal phrase, not a sentence.

▶ Mary is suffering from agoraphobia/, ~~A~~ fear of the

outside world.

A fear of the outside world is an appositive phrase, not a sentence.

▶ It has been said that there are only three

indigenous American art forms/: ~~J~~azz, musical

comedy, and soap operas.

Clearly the list is not a sentence. Notice how easily a colon corrects the problem. (See p. 61.)

If the fragmented phrase cannot be attached to a nearby sentence, turn the phrase into a sentence. You may need to add a subject, a verb, or both.

▶ If Eric doesn't get his way, he goes into a fit of rage.
 he lies
For example, ~~lying~~ on the floor screaming or
 opens ^ *slams*
~~opening~~ the cabinet doors and then ~~slamming~~

them shut.

The writer corrected this fragment by adding a subject — *he* — and substituting verbs for the verbals *lying*, *opening*, and *slamming*.

14c. Acceptable fragments

Skilled writers occasionally use sentence fragments for emphasis. In the following passage, Richard Rodriguez uses a fragment (italicized) to draw attention to his mother.

Following the dramatic Americanization of their children, even my parents grew more publicly confident. *Especially my mother*. She learned the names of all the people on our block.

— *Hunger of Memory*

Although fragments are sometimes appropriate, writers and readers do not always agree on when they are appropriate. Therefore, you will find it safer to write in complete sentences.

15. Revise run-on sentences.

Run-on sentences are independent clauses that have not been joined correctly. An independent clause is a word group that does or could stand alone as a sentence. When two or more independent clauses appear in one sentence, they must be joined in one of these ways:

—with a comma and a coordinating conjunction (*and, but, or, nor, for, so, yet*)

—with a semicolon (or occasionally a colon or a dash)

There are two types of run-on sentences. When a writer puts no mark of punctuation and no coordinating conjunction between independent clauses, the result is called a fused sentence.

FUSED Gestures are a means of communication for everyone they are essential for the hearing-impaired.

A far more common type of run-on sentence is the comma splice — two or more independent clauses joined by a comma without a coordinating conjunction. In some comma splices, the comma appears alone.

COMMA SPLICE Gestures are a means of communication for everyone, they are essential for the hearing-impaired.

In other comma splices, the comma is accompanied by a joining word that is *not* a coordinating conjunction. There are only seven coordinating conjunctions in English: *and, but, or, nor, for, so, yet*.

COMMA SPLICE Gestures are a means of communication for everyone, however, they are essential for the hearing-impaired.

The word *however* is a conjunctive adverb, not a coordinating conjunction. When used to join independent clauses, a conjunctive adverb must be preceded by a semicolon.

To correct a run-on sentence, you have four choices:

1. Use a comma and a coordinating conjunction.
2. Use a semicolon (or, if appropriate, a colon or a dash).
3. Make the clauses into separate sentences.
4. Restructure the sentence, perhaps by subordinating one of the clauses.

One of these revision techniques will usually work better than the others for a particular sentence. The fourth technique, the one requiring the most extensive revision, is frequently the most effective.

▶ Gestures are a means of communication for
but
everyone, they are essential for the hearing-
^
impaired.

▶ Gestures are a means of communication for
;
everyone/ they are essential for the hearing-
^
impaired.

▶ Gestures are a means of communication for
T
everyone/. they are essential for the hearing-
^
impaired.

Although gestures
▶ ~~Gestures~~ are a means of communication for
^
everyone, they are essential for the hearing-

impaired.

15a. Revision with a comma and a coordinating conjunction

When a coordinating conjunction (*and, but, or, nor, for, so, yet*) joins independent clauses, it is usually preceded by a comma.

▶ Most of his contemporaries had made plans for

but

their retirement, ˄ Tom had not.

15b. Revision with a semicolon
When the independent clauses are closely related and their relation is clear without a coordinating conjunction, a semicolon is an acceptable method of revision.

▶ The suburbs seemed cold/ ; ˄ they lacked the

warmth and excitement of our Italian neighborhood.

A semicolon is required between independent clauses that have been linked with a conjunctive adverb such as *however* or *therefore* or a transitional phrase such as *in fact* or *of course*. (See p. 60 for a more complete list.)

▶ The timber wolf looks like a large German

shepherd/ ; ˄ however, the wolf has longer legs,

larger feet, and a wider head.

15c. Revision by separating sentences
If both independent clauses are long — or if one is a question and the other is not — consider making them separate sentences.

▶ Why should we pay taxes to support public trans-

W

portation/ ? ˄ we prefer to save energy by carpooling.

15d. Revision by restructuring the sentence
For sentence variety, consider restructuring the sentence, perhaps by turning one of the independent clauses into a subordinate clause or phrase.

▶ It was obvious that Paula had been out walking in

because

the woods ˄ her boots were covered with mud and

leaves.

▶ Nuclear power plants produce energy by fission,

~~it is~~ a process that generates radioactive waste.

16. If English is not your native language, check for common ESL problems.

This section of *A Pocket Style Manual* has a special audience: speakers of English as a second language (ESL) who have learned English but continue to have difficulty with a few troublesome features of the language.

16a. Articles

The definite article *the* and the indefinite articles *a* and *an* signal that a noun is about to appear. The noun may follow the article immediately or modifiers may intervene.

> *the cat, the* black *cat*
> *a sunset, a* spectacular *sunset*
> *an apple, an* appetizing *apple*

When to use a (or an). Use *a* or *an* with singular count nouns whose specific identity is not known to the reader. Count nouns refer to persons, places, or things that can be counted: *one girl, two girls; one city, three cities.*

▶ Mary Beth arrived in ^*a*^ limousine.

▶ The biology student looked for ^*an*^ insect like the one

in his textbook.

A (or *an*) usually means "one among many" but can also mean "any one."

NOTE: *A* is used before a consonant sound: *a banana, a happy child. An* is used before a vowel sound: *an eggplant, an honorable person.* See the Glossary of Usage.

When not to use a (or an). *A* (or *an*) is not used to mark noncount nouns. Noncount nouns refer to entities or abstractions that cannot be counted: *water, silver, sugar, furniture, patience.* (See below for a fuller list.)

▶ Claudia asked her mother for ~~an~~ advice.

If you want to express an amount of something designated by a noncount noun, you can often add a quantifier in front of it: *a quart of milk, an ounce of gold, a piece of furniture.*

NOTE: A few noncount nouns may also be used as count nouns: *Bill loves lemonade; Bill offered me a lemonade.*

> **COMMONLY USED NONCOUNT NOUNS**
>
> *Food and drink*: bacon, beef, bread, broccoli, butter, cabbage, candy, cauliflower, celery, cereal, cheese, chicken, chocolate, coffee, corn, cream, fish, flour, fruit, ice cream, lemonade, lettuce, meat, milk, oil, pasta, rice, salt, spinach, sugar, tea, water, wine, yogurt
>
> *Nonfood substances*: air, cement, coal, dirt, gasoline, gold, paper, petroleum, plastic, rain, silver, snow, soap, steel, wood, wool
>
> *Abstract nouns*: advice, anger, beauty, confidence, courage, employment, fun, happiness, health, honesty, information, intelligence, knowledge, love, poverty, satisfaction, truth, wealth
>
> *Other*: biology (and other areas of study), clothing, equipment, furniture, homework, jewelry, luggage, lumber, machinery, mail, money, news, poetry, pollution, research, scenery, traffic, transportation, violence, weather, work

When to use the. Use the definite article *the* with most nouns whose specific identity is known to the reader. Usually the identity will be clear for one of these reasons:

1. The noun has been previously mentioned.
2. A word group following the noun restricts its identity.
3. The context or situation makes the noun's identity clear.

▶ A truck loaded with dynamite cut in front of our
the
van. When truck skidded a few seconds later, we
^
almost plowed into it.

The noun *truck* is preceded by *A* when it is first mentioned. When the noun is mentioned again, it is preceded by *the* since readers now know the specific truck being discussed.

the
▶ Bob warned me that gun on the top shelf of the
^
cupboard was loaded.

The phrase *on the top shelf of the cupboard* identifies the specific gun.

the
▶ Please don't slam door when you leave.
^

Both the speaker and the listener know which door is meant.

When not to use the. Do not use *the* with plural or noncount nouns meaning "all" or "in general."

F
▶ ~~The~~ fountains are an expensive element of

landscape design.

▶ In some parts of the world, ~~the~~ rice is preferred to

all other grains.

Although there are many exceptions, do not use *the* with most singular proper nouns: names of persons (Jessica Webner); names of streets, squares, parks, cities, and states (Prospect Street, Union Square, Denali National Park, Miami, Idaho); names of continents and most countries (South America, Italy); and names of bays and single lakes, mountains, and islands (Tampa Bay, Lake Geneva, Mount Everest, Crete).

Exceptions to this rule include names of large regions, deserts, and peninsulas (the East Coast, the Sahara, the Iberian Peninsula) and names of oceans, seas, gulfs, canals, and rivers (the Pacific, the Dead Sea, the Persian Gulf, the Panama Canal, the Amazon).

NOTE: *The* is used to mark plural proper nouns: the United Nations, the Finger Lakes, the Andes, the Bahamas.

16b. Helping verbs and main verbs

Only certain combinations of helping verbs and main verbs make sense in English. The correct combinations are discussed in this section, after the following review of helping verbs and main verbs.

Review. Helping verbs always appear before main verbs.

HV MV   HV   MV
We *will leave* at noon. *Do* you *want* a ride?

Some helping verbs—*have, do,* and *be*—change form to indicate tenses; others, known as modals, do not.

> **HELPING VERBS**
>
> *Forms of* do: do, does, did
>
> *Forms of* have: have, has, had
>
> *Forms of* be: be, am, is, are, was, were, being, been
>
> *Modals*: can, could, may, might, must, shall, should, will, would (*also* ought to)

Every main verb has five forms (except *be*, which has eight). The following list shows these forms for the regular verb *help* and the irregular verb *give*. (See pp. 24–25 for a list of common irregular verbs.)

BASE FORM	help, give
-S FORM	helps, gives
PAST TENSE	helped, gave
PAST PARTICIPLE	helped, given
PRESENT PARTICIPLE	helping, giving

Modal + base form. After the modals *can, could, may, might, must, shall, should, will,* and *would,* use the base form of the verb.

▶ Geologists predicted that a minor earthquake

    would occur~~s~~ along the Santa Ana fault line.

> We could ~~spoke~~ ^speak^ Spanish when we were young.

Do, does, *or* **did** + *base form.* After helping verbs that are a form of *do*, use the base form of the verb.

> Mariko does not want~~s~~ any more dessert.

> Did Janice ~~bought~~ ^buy^ the gift for Katherine?

Have, has, *or* **had** + *past participle.* To form one of the perfect tenses, use *have, has,* or *had* followed by a past participle (usually ending in *-ed, -d, -en, -n,* or *-t*). (See perfect tenses, pp. 26–27.)

> Many churches have ~~offer~~ ^offered^ shelter to the homeless.

> An-Mei has not ~~speaking~~ ^spoken^ Chinese since she was a child.

Form of **be** + *present participle.* To express an action in progress, use *am, is, are, was, were, be,* or *been* followed by a present participle (the *-ing* form of the verb).

> Because it is a clear night, I am ~~turn~~ ^turning^ my telescope to the constellation Cassiopeia.

> Uncle Roy was ~~driven~~ ^driving^ a brand-new red Corvette.

The helping verbs *be* and *been* must be preceded by other helping verbs. See the progressive forms listed on page 27.

CAUTION: Certain verbs are not normally used in the progressive sense in English. In general, these verbs express a state of being or mental activity, not a dynamic action. Common examples are *appear, believe, have, hear, know, like, need, see, seem, taste, think, understand,* and *want.*

> I ~~am wanting~~ ^want^ to see August Wilson's *Seven Guitars* at Arena Stage.

***Form of* be + *past participle*.** To form the passive voice, use *am, are, was, were, being, be,* or *been* followed by a past participle (usually ending in *-ed, -d, -en, -n,* or *-t*). When a sentence is written in the passive voice, the subject of the sentence receives the action instead of doing it. (See p. 28.)

▶ *Bleak House* was ~~write~~ by Charles Dickens.
              ^written^

▶ The scientists were ~~honor~~ for their work with
                 ^honored^

    endangered species.

In the passive voice, the helping verb *be* must be preceded by a modal: *Senator Dixon will be defeated. Being* must be preceded by *am, is, are, was,* or *were: The child was being teased. Been* must be preceded by *have, has,* or *had: I have been invited to a party.*

CAUTION: Although they may seem to have passive meanings, verbs such as *occur, happen, sleep, die,* and *fall* may not be used to form the passive voice because they are intransitive. Only transitive verbs, those that take direct objects, may be used to form the passive voice.

▶ The earthquake ~~was~~ occurred last Friday.

16c. Omitted subjects, expletives, or verbs

Some languages allow omission of subjects, expletives, or verbs in certain contexts. English does not.

English requires a subject for all sentences except imperatives, in which the subject *you* is understood (*Give to the poor*). If your native language allows the omission of an explicit subject, be especially alert to this requirement in English.

▶ ~~Have~~ a large collection of baseball cards.
  I have

▶ My brother is very bright; could read a book
                             he

    before he started school.

When the subject has been moved from its normal position before the verb, English sometimes requires an expletive (*there* or *it*) at the beginning of the sentence or clause.

▶ As you know, ~~are~~ many religious sects in India.
there ^

▶ ~~Is~~ healthy to eat fruit and grains.
It is ^

The subjects of these sentences are *sects* and *to eat fruit and grains*.

Although some languages allow the omission of the verb when the meaning is clear without it, English does not.

▶ Powell Street in San Francisco very steep.
is ^

16d. Repeated subjects or objects

English does not allow a subject to be repeated in its own clause. This is true even if a word group intervenes between the subject and the verb.

▶ The painting that had been stolen ~~it~~ was found.

The pronoun *it* repeats the subject *painting*.

In some languages an object is repeated later in the adjective clause in which it appears; in English, such repetitions are not allowed. Adjective clauses usually begin with *who, whom, whose, which,* or *that,* and these words always serve a grammatical function within the clauses they introduce. Another word in the clause cannot also serve that same function.

▶ The puppy ran after the taxi that we were riding

in. ~~it.~~
^

The relative pronoun *that* is the object of the preposition *in,* so the object *it* is not allowed.

Even when the relative pronoun has been omitted, do not add another word with its same function.

▶ The puppy ran after the taxi we were riding in. ~~it.~~
^

The relative pronoun *that* is understood.

Punctuation

17. The comma

The comma was invented to help readers. Without it, sentence parts can collide into one another unexpectedly, causing misreadings.

CONFUSING If you cook Elmer will do the dishes.

CONFUSING While we were eating a rattlesnake
                approached our campsite.

Add commas in the logical places (after *cook* and *eating*), and suddenly all is clear. No longer is Elmer being cooked, the rattlesnake being eaten.

Various rules have evolved to prevent such misreadings and to guide readers through complex grammatical structures. According to most experts, you should use a comma in the following situations.

17a. Before a coordinating conjunction joining independent clauses

When a coordinating conjunction connects two or more independent clauses — word groups that could stand alone as separate sentences — a comma must precede it. There are seven coordinating conjunctions in English: *and, but, or, nor, for, so,* and *yet.*

A comma tells readers that one independent clause has come to a close and that another is about to begin.

▶ Nearly everyone has heard of love at first sight‸

    but I fell in love at first dance.

EXCEPTION: If the two independent clauses are short and there is no danger of misreading, the comma may be omitted.

    The plane took off and we were on our way.

CAUTION: Do *not* use a comma to separate compound elements that are not independent clauses. See page 58.

17b. After an introductory word group

Use a comma after an introductory adverb clause, prepositional phrase, or participial phrase. A comma tells readers that the introductory word group has come to a close and that the main part of the sentence is about to begin.

▶ When Irwin was ready to eat, his cat jumped onto the table.

▶ Near a small stream at the bottom of the canyon, we discovered an abandoned shelter.

▶ Excited about the move, Alice and Don began packing their books.

EXCEPTION: The comma may be omitted after a short clause or phrase if there is no danger of misreading.

In no time we were at 2,800 feet.

17c. Between items in a series

Use a comma between all items in a series, including the last two.

▶ Anne Frank and thousands like her were forced to hide in attics, cellars, and secret rooms.

Although some writers view the comma between the last two items as optional, most experts advise using it because its omission can result in ambiguity or misreading.

17d. Between coordinate adjectives

Use a comma between coordinate adjectives, those that each modify a noun separately.

▶ Patients with severe, irreversible brain damage should not be put on life support systems.

Adjectives are coordinate if they can be connected with *and*: *severe and irreversible*.

CAUTION: Do not use a comma between cumulative adjectives, those that do not each modify the noun separately.

> *Three large gray* shapes moved slowly toward us.

Adjectives are cumulative if they cannot be connected with *and*. It would be very odd to say *three and large and gray shapes*.

17e. To set off a nonrestrictive element

A *restrictive* element restricts the meaning of the word it modifies and is therefore essential to the meaning of the sentence. It is not set off with commas. A *nonrestrictive* element describes a word whose meaning already is clear. It is not essential to the meaning of the sentence and is set off with commas.

RESTRICTIVE

For camp the children needed clothes *that were washable*.

NONRESTRICTIVE

For camp the children needed sturdy shoes, *which were expensive*.

If you remove a restrictive element from a sentence, the meaning changes significantly, becoming more general than intended. The writer of the first sample sentence does not mean that the children needed clothes in general. The meaning is more restricted: The children needed *washable* clothes.

If you remove a nonrestrictive element from a sentence, the meaning does not change significantly. Some meaning is lost, to be sure, but the defining characteristics of the person or thing described remain the same as before. The children needed *sturdy shoes*, and these happened to be expensive.

Elements that may be restrictive or nonrestrictive include adjective clauses, adjective phrases, and appositives.

Adjective clauses. Adjective clauses, which usually follow the noun or pronoun they describe, begin with a relative pronoun (*who, whom, whose, which, that*) or a relative adverb (*when, where*). When an adjective clause is nonrestrictive, set it off with commas; when it is restrictive, omit the commas.

NONRESTRICTIVE CLAUSE

▶ The United States Coast Survey, which was established in 1807, was the first scientific agency in this country.

RESTRICTIVE CLAUSE

▶ A corporation/that has government contracts/must maintain careful personnel records.

NOTE: Use *that* only with restrictive clauses. Many writers use *which* only with nonrestrictive clauses, but usage varies.

Adjective phrases. Prepositional or verbal phrases functioning as adjectives may be restrictive or nonrestrictive. Nonrestrictive phrases are set off with commas; restrictive phrases are not.

NONRESTRICTIVE PHRASE

▶ The helicopter, with its 100,000-candlepower spotlight illuminating the area, circled above.

RESTRICTIVE PHRASE

▶ One corner of the attic was filled with newspapers/ dating from the turn of the century.

Appositives. An appositive is a noun or pronoun that renames a nearby noun. Nonrestrictive appositives are set off with commas; restrictive appositives are not.

NONRESTRICTIVE APPOSITIVE

▶ Darwin's most important book, *On the Origin of Species*, was the result of many years of research.

RESTRICTIVE APPOSITIVE

▶ The song/ "Fire It Up/" was blasted out of amplifiers ten feet tall.

17f. To set off transitional and parenthetical expressions, absolute phrases, and contrasted elements

Transitional expressions. Transitional expressions serve as bridges between sentences or parts of sentences. They include conjunctive adverbs such as *however*, *therefore*, and *moreover* and transitional phrases such as *for example* and *as a matter of fact*. For a more complete list, see page 60.

When a transitional expression appears between independent clauses in a compound sentence, it is preceded by a semicolon and usually followed by a comma.

▶ Minh did not understand our language; moreover, he was unfamiliar with our customs.

When a transitional expression appears at the beginning of a sentence or in the middle of an independent clause, it is usually set off with commas.

▶ As a matter of fact, American football was established by fans who wanted to play a more organized game of rugby.

▶ The prospective babysitter looked very promising; she was busy, however, throughout January.

Parenthetical expressions. Expressions that are distinctly parenthetical, interrupting the flow of a sentence, should be set off with commas.

▶ Evolution, so far as we know, does not work this way.

Absolute phrases. An absolute phrase, which modifies the whole sentence, should be set off with commas.

▶ His tennis game at last perfected, Chris won the cup.

Contrasted elements. Sharp contrasts beginning with words such as *not* and *unlike* are set off with commas.

▶ Celia, unlike Robert, had no loathing for dance

contests.

17g. To set off nouns of direct address, the words *yes* and *no*, interrogative tags, and mild interjections

▶ Forgive us, Dr. Spock, for spanking Brian.

▶ Yes, the loan will probably be approved.

▶ The film was faithful to the book, wasn't it?

▶ Well, cases like this are difficult to decide.

17h. To set off direct quotations introduced with expressions such as *he said*

▶ Naturalist Arthur Cleveland Bent remarked, "In

part the peregrine declined unnoticed because it is

not adorable."

17i. With dates, addresses, titles

Dates. In dates, the year is set off from the rest of the sentence with commas.

▶ On December 12, 1890, orders were sent out for

the arrest of Sitting Bull.

EXCEPTIONS: Commas are not needed if the date is inverted or if only the month and year are given: *The deadline is 15 April 1998. May 1996 was a surprisingly cold month.*

Addresses. The elements of an address or place name are followed by commas. A zip code, however, is not preceded by a comma.

no ,

▶ Greg lived at 708 Spring Street, Washington,

Illinois 61571.

Titles. If a title follows a name, separate it from the rest of the sentence with a pair of commas.

▶ Sandra Barnes, M.D., performed the surgery.

17j. Misuses of the comma

Do not use commas unless you have a good reason for using them. In particular, avoid using the comma in the following situations.

BETWEEN COMPOUND ELEMENTS THAT ARE NOT INDEPENDENT CLAUSES

▶ Marie Curie discovered radium/ and later applied

her work on radioactivity to medicine.

TO SEPARATE A VERB FROM ITS SUBJECT

▶ Zoos large enough to give the animals freedom to

roam/ are becoming more popular.

BETWEEN CUMULATIVE ADJECTIVES (See p. 53.)

▶ Joyce was wearing a slinky/ red silk gown.

TO SET OFF RESTRICTIVE ELEMENTS (See pp. 54–55.)

▶ Drivers/ who think they own the road/ make cycling

a dangerous sport.

AFTER A COORDINATING CONJUNCTION

▶ Occasionally soap operas are live, but/ more often

they are taped.

AFTER *SUCH AS* OR *LIKE*

▶ Plants such as/ begonias and impatiens add color

to a shady garden.

BEFORE *THAN*

▶ Touring Crete was more thrilling for us╱ than
visiting the Greek islands frequented by the jet set.

BEFORE A PARENTHESIS

▶ At MCI Sylvia began at the bottom╱ (with only a
cubicle and a swivel chair), but within five years
she had been promoted to supervisor.

TO SET OFF AN INDIRECT (REPORTED) QUOTATION

▶ Samuel Goldwyn once, said╱ that a verbal contract
isn't worth the paper it's written on.

WITH A QUESTION MARK OR AN EXCLAMATION POINT

▶ "Why don't you try it?╱ " she coaxed.

18. The semicolon and the colon

18a. The semicolon

The semicolon is used between independent clauses
not joined by a coordinating conjunction. It can also be
used between items in a series containing internal
punctuation.

The semicolon is never used between elements of
unequal grammatical rank.

Between independent clauses.   When related independent clauses appear in one sentence, they are ordinarily connected with a comma and a coordinating conjunction (*and, but, or, nor, for, so, yet*). The coordinating
conjunction expresses the relation between the clauses.
If the relation is clear without a conjunction, a writer
may choose to connect the clauses with a semicolon
instead.

> Injustice is relatively easy to bear; what stings is
> justice.   — H. L. Mencken

A writer may also choose to connect the clauses with a semicolon and a conjunctive adverb such as *however* or *therefore* or a transitional phrase such as *for example* or *in fact*.

> He swallowed a lot of wisdom; however, it seemed as if all of it had gone down the wrong way.
>
> — G. C. Lichtenberg

CONJUNCTIVE ADVERBS

accordingly, also, anyway, besides, certainly, consequently, conversely, finally, furthermore, hence, however, incidentally, indeed, instead, likewise, meanwhile, moreover, nevertheless, next, nonetheless, otherwise, similarly, specifically, still, subsequently, then, therefore, thus

TRANSITIONAL PHRASES

after all, as a matter of fact, as a result, at any rate, at the same time, even so, for example, for instance, in addition, in conclusion, in fact, in other words, in the first place, on the contrary, on the other hand

CAUTION: A semicolon must be used whenever a coordinating conjunction has been omitted between independent clauses. To use merely a comma — or to use a comma and a conjunctive adverb or transitional expression — creates an error known as a comma splice. (See pp. 41–42.)

▶ Some educators believe that African American history should be taught in separate courses/ others prefer to see it integrated into survey courses.

Between items in a series containing internal punctuation. Ordinarily, items in a series are separated by commas. If one or more of the items contains internal punctuation, however, a writer may use semicolons instead.

> The only sensible ends of literature are first, the pleasurable toil of writing; second, the gratification of one's family and friends; and lastly, the solid cash.
>
> — Nathaniel Hawthorne

Misuses of the semicolon. Do not use a semicolon in the following situations.

BETWEEN A SUBORDINATE CLAUSE AND THE REST OF THE SENTENCE

▶ Unless you brush your teeth within ten or fifteen minutes after eating⅄ brushing does almost no good.

BETWEEN AN APPOSITIVE AND THE WORD IT REFERS TO

▶ Another delicious dish is the chef's special⅄ a roasted duck stuffed with wild rice.

TO INTRODUCE A LIST

▶ Some of my favorite artists are featured on *Red, Hot, and Blue*⅄ the Neville Brothers, Annie Lennox, and k. d. lang.

BETWEEN INDEPENDENT CLAUSES JOINED BY *AND*, *BUT*, *OR*, *NOR*, *FOR*, *SO*, OR *YET*

▶ Five of the applicants had worked with spread-sheets⅄ but only one was familiar with database management.

18b. The colon

The colon is used after an independent clause to call attention to the words that follow it. The colon also has certain conventional uses.

To call attention to the words that follow it. After an independent clause, a writer may use a colon to direct the reader's attention to a list, an appositive, or a quotation.

   A LIST

   The routine includes the following: twenty knee bends, fifty leg lifts, and five minutes of running in place.

AN APPOSITIVE

There are only three seasons here: winter, July, and August.

A QUOTATION

Consider the words of John F. Kennedy: "Ask not what your country can do for you; ask what you can do for your country."

For other ways of introducing quotations, see pages 67–68.

A colon may also be used between independent clauses if the second summarizes or explains the first.

Minds are like parachutes: They function only when open.

Conventional uses. Use a colon after the salutation in a formal letter, to indicate hours and minutes, to show proportions, between a title and subtitle, and to separate city and publisher in bibliographic entries.

Dear Sir or Madam:

5:30 P.M. (or p.m.)

The ratio of women to men was 2:1.

The Glory of Hera: Greek Mythology and the Greek Family

Boston: Bedford, 1997

NOTE: In biblical references, a colon is ordinarily used between chapter and verse (Luke 2:14). The Modern Language Association recommends a period (Luke 2.14).

Misuses of the colon. A colon must be preceded by an independent clause. Therefore, avoid using it in the following situations.

BETWEEN A VERB AND ITS OBJECT OR COMPLEMENT

▶ Some important vitamins found in vegetables are:

vitamin A, thiamine, niacin, and vitamin C.

BETWEEN A PREPOSITION AND ITS OBJECT

▶ The heart's two pumps each consist of/ an upper
chamber, or atrium, and a lower chamber, or
ventricle.

AFTER *SUCH AS, INCLUDING,* **OR** *FOR EXAMPLE*

▶ The trees on campus include fine Japanese
specimens such as/ black pines, ginkgos, and
cutleaf maples.

19. The apostrophe

The apostrophe is used to indicate possession and to
mark contractions. In addition, it has a few conventional uses.

19a. To indicate possession

The apostrophe is used to indicate that a noun is possessive. Possessive nouns usually indicate ownership,
as in *Tim's hat* or *the editor's desk*. Frequently, however,
ownership is only loosely implied: *the tree's roots, a
day's work*. If you are not sure whether a noun is possessive, try turning it into an *of* phrase: *the roots of the
tree, the work of a day*.

When to add -'s. Add -'s if the noun does not end in
-*s* or if the noun is singular and ends in -*s*.

A crocodile's life span is about thirteen years.

Thank you for refunding the children's money.

Lois's sister spent last year in India.

EXCEPTION: If pronunciation would be awkward with
the added -'s, some writers use only the apostrophe:
Sophocles' plays are among my favorites. Either use is
acceptable.

When to add only an apostrophe. If the noun is plural and ends in -*s*, add only an apostrophe.

> Both diplomats' briefcases were stolen.

Joint possession. To show joint possession, use -'*s* (or -*s*') with the last noun only; to show individual possession, make all nouns possessive.

> Have you seen Joyce and Greg's new camper?

> Hernando's and Maria's expectations were quite different.

Compound nouns. If a noun is compound, use -'*s* (or -*s*') with the last element.

> Her father-in-law's sculpture won first place.

Indefinite pronouns such as someone. Use -'*s* to indicate that an indefinite pronoun is possessive. Indefinite pronouns refer to no specific person or thing: *everyone*, *someone*, *no one*, and so on.

> Someone's raincoat has been left behind.

19b. To mark contractions

In a contraction, an apostrophe takes the place of missing letters.

> It's a shame that Frank can't go on the tour.

It's stands for *it is*, *can't* for *cannot*.
The apostrophe is also used to mark the omission of the first two digits of a year (*the class of '96*) or years (*the '60s generation*).

19c. Conventional uses

An apostrophe may be used to pluralize numbers mentioned as numbers, letters mentioned as letters, words mentioned as words, and abbreviations.

> Peggy skated nearly perfect figure 8's.

> Two large red *J*'s were painted on the door.

> We've heard enough *maybe*'s.

> You must ask to see their I.D.'s.

EXCEPTION: An -*s* alone is often added to the years in a decade: *the 1990s.*

19d. Misuses of the apostrophe
Do not use an apostrophe in the following situations.

WITH NOUNS THAT ARE NOT POSSESSIVE
▶ Some ~~outpatient's~~ are given special parking

    outpatients

permits.

IN THE POSSESSIVE PRONOUNS *ITS*, *WHOSE*, *HIS*, *HERS*, *OURS*, *YOURS*, **AND** *THEIRS*
▶ Each area has ~~it's~~ own conference room.

    its

    It's means *it is.* The possessive pronoun *its* contains no apostrophe despite the fact that it is possessive.

20. Quotation marks

Quotation marks are used to enclose direct quotations. They are also used around some titles and to set off words used as words.

20a. To enclose direct quotations
Direct quotations of a person's words, whether spoken or written, must be in quotation marks.

> "A foolish consistency is the hobgoblin of little minds," wrote Ralph Waldo Emerson.

EXCEPTION: When a long quotation has been set off from the text by indenting, quotation marks are not needed. See page 98.

    Use single quotation marks to enclose a quotation within a quotation.

> According to Paul Eliott, Eskimo hunters "chant an ancient magic song to the seal they are after: 'Beast of the sea! Come and place yourself before me in the early morning!'"

20b. Around titles of short works

Use quotation marks around titles of newspaper and magazine articles, poems, short stories, songs, episodes of television and radio programs, and chapters or subdivisions of books.

> The poem "Mother to Son" is by Langston Hughes.

NOTE: Titles of books, plays, and films and names of magazines and newspapers are put in italics or underlined. See pages 79–80.

20c. To set off words used as words

Although words used as words are ordinarily underlined to indicate italics, quotation marks are also acceptable.

> The words "flaunt" and "flout" are frequently confused.

> The words *flaunt* and *flout* are frequently confused.

20d. Other punctuation with quotation marks

This section describes the conventions to observe in placing various marks of punctuation inside or outside quotation marks. It also explains how to punctuate when introducing quoted material.

Periods and commas. Place periods and commas inside quotation marks.

> "This is a stick-up," said the well-dressed young couple. "We want all your money."

This rule applies to single and double quotation marks, and it applies to all uses of quotation marks.

NOTE: MLA parenthetical citations are an exception to this rule. Put the parenthetical citation after the quotation mark and before the period: *According to Kane, "Pollution has become a serious problem in most of our national parks"* (5). See pages 103–07.

Colons and semicolons. Put colons and semicolons outside quotation marks.

Harold wrote, "I regret that I cannot attend the AIDS fundraiser"; his letter, however, contained a contribution.

Question marks and exclamation points. Put question marks and exclamation points inside quotation marks unless they apply to the sentence as a whole.

Contrary to tradition, bedtime at my house is marked by "Mommy, can I tell you a story now?"

Have you heard the old proverb "Do not climb the hill until you reach it"?

In the first sentence, the question mark applies only to the quoted question. In the second sentence, the question mark applies to the whole sentence.

NOTE: MLA parenthetical citations create a special problem. According to MLA, the question mark or exclamation point should appear before the quotation mark, and a period should follow the parenthetical citation: *Rosie Thomas asks, "Is nothing in life ever straight and clear, the way children see it?"* (77).

Introducing quoted material. After a word group introducing a quotation, use a colon, a comma, or no punctuation at all, whichever is appropriate in context.

If a quotation has been formally introduced, a colon is appropriate. A formal introduction is a full independent clause, not just an expression such as *he said* or *she remarked*.

Morrow views personal ads as an art form: "The personal ad is like haiku of self-celebration, a brief solo played on one's own horn."

If a quotation is introduced or followed by an expression such as *he said* or *she remarked*, use a comma.

Robert Frost said, "You can be a little ungrammatical if you come from the right part of the country."

"You can be a little ungrammatical if you come from the right part of the country," said Robert Frost.

When you blend a quotation into your own sentence, use either a comma or no punctuation, depend ing on the way in which the quotation fits into the sentence structure.

> The future champion could, as he put it, "float like a butterfly and sting like a bee."

> Hudson noted that the prisoners escaped "by squeezing through a tiny window eighteen feet above the floor of their cell."

If a quotation appears at the beginning of a sentence, set it off with a comma unless the quotation ends with a question mark or an exclamation point.

> "We shot them like dogs," boasted Davy Crockett, who was among Jackson's troops.

> "What is it?" I asked, bracing myself.

If a quoted sentence is interrupted by explanatory words, use commas to set off the explanatory words.

> "A great many people think they are thinking," wrote William James, "when they are merely rearranging their prejudices."

If two successive quoted sentences from the same source are interrupted by explanatory words, use a comma before the explanatory words and a period after them.

> "I was a flop as a daily reporter," admitted E.B. White. "Every piece had to be a masterpiece — and before you knew it, Tuesday was Wednesday."

20e. Misuses of quotation marks

Do not use quotation marks to draw attention to familiar slang, to disown trite expressions, or to justify an attempt at humor.

▶ Between Thanksgiving and Super Bowl Sunday,

many American wives become/"football widows."

Do not use quotation marks around indirect quotations. Indirect quotations report a person's words instead of quoting them directly.

▶ After leaving the scene of the domestic quarrel,

the officer said that/"he was due for a coffee break."

Do not use quotation marks around the title of your own essay.

21. Other marks

21a. The period

Use a period to end all sentences except direct questions or genuine exclamations. Use a period, not a question mark, for an indirect question — that is, a reported question.

> Celia asked whether the picnic would be canceled.

A period is conventionally used in abbreviations such as the following.

Mr.	B.A.	B.C.	i.e.	A.M. (or a.m.)
Ms.	Ph.D.	B.C.E.	e.g.	P.M. (or p.m.)
Dr.	R.N.	A.D.	etc.	

A period is not used with U.S. Postal Service abbreviations for states: MD, TX, CA.

Ordinarily a period is not used in abbreviations of organization names.

NATO	IRS	AFL-CIO	FCC
USA (or	NAACP	GATT	AOL
U.S.A.)	UCLA	NBA	NIH

Usage varies, however. When in doubt, consult a dictionary, a style manual, or a publication by the agency in question. Even the yellow pages can help.

NOTE: If a sentence ends with a period marking an abbreviation, do not add a second period.

21b. The question mark

Use a question mark after a direct question.

> What is the horsepower of a 747 engine?

If a polite request is written in the form of a question, you may use a question mark, though usage varies.

> Would you please send me your catalog of lilies?

CAUTION: Use a period, not a question mark, after an indirect question, one that is reported rather than asked directly.

> He asked me where the nearest pastry shop was.

21c. The exclamation point

Use an exclamation point after a sentence that expresses exceptional feeling or deserves special emphasis.

> The medic shook me and kept yelling, "He's dead! He's dead! Can't you see that?"

CAUTION: Do not overuse the exclamation point.

> ▶ In the fisherman's memory the fish lives on,
>
> increasing in length and weight with each passing
>
> year, until at last it is big enough to shade a
>
> fishing boat̸**.**
>   ^

This sentence doesn't need to be pumped up with an exclamation point. It is emphatic enough without it.

21d. The dash

The dash may be used to set off material that deserves special emphasis. When typing, use two hyphens to form a dash (- -), with no spaces before or after them.

Use a dash to introduce a list, a restatement, an amplification, or a dramatic shift in tone or thought.

> Along the wall are the bulk liquids — sesame seed oil, honey, safflower oil, and half-liquid peanut butter.

> Consider the amount of sugar in the average person's diet — 104 pounds per year.

> Kiere took a few steps back, came running full speed, kicked a mighty kick — and missed the ball completely.

In the first two examples, the writer could also use a colon. (See p. 61.) The colon is more formal than the dash and not quite as dramatic.

Use a pair of dashes to set off parenthetical material that deserves special emphasis or to set off an appositive that contains commas.

Everything that went wrong — from the peeping
Tom at her window to my head-on collision — was
blamed on our move.

In my hometown the basic needs of people —
food, clothing, and shelter — are less costly than
in Denver.

CAUTION: Unless you have a specific reason for using
the dash, avoid it. Unnecessary dashes create a choppy
effect.

▶ Seeing that our young people learn to use

computers makes good sense. Herding them ~~/~~

sheeplike ~~/~~ into computer technology does not.

21e. Parentheses

Use parentheses to enclose supplemental material, minor digressions, and afterthoughts.

After taking her temperature, pulse, and blood
pressure (routine vital signs), the nurse made
Becky comfortable.

Use parentheses to enclose letters or numbers labeling
items in a series.

There are three points of etiquette in poker:
(1) always allow someone to cut the cards,
(2) don't forget to ante up, and (3) never stack
your chips.

CAUTION: Do not overuse parentheses. Often a sentence reads more gracefully without them.

from ten to fifty million
▶ Researchers have said that ~~ten million (estimates~~
       ^

~~run as high as fifty million)~~ Americans have

hypoglycemia.

21f. Brackets

Use brackets to enclose any words or phrases inserted
into an otherwise word-for-word quotation.

Audubon reports that "if there are not enough
young to balance deaths, the end of the species
[California condor] is inevitable."

The *Audubon* article did not contain the words *California condor* in the sentence quoted.

The Latin word *sic* in brackets indicates that an error in a quoted sentence appears in the original source.

> According to the review, Kistler's performance was brilliant, "exceding [*sic*] the expectations of even her most loyal fans."

21g. The ellipsis mark

Use an ellipsis mark, three spaced periods, to indicate that you have deleted material from an otherwise word-for-word quotation.

> Reuben reports that "when the amount of cholesterol circulating in the blood rises over . . . 300 milligrams per 100, the chances of a heart attack increase dramatically."

If you delete a full sentence or more in the middle of a quoted passage, use a period before the three ellipsis dots.

CAUTION: Do not use the ellipsis mark at the beginning of a quotation; do not use it at the end of a quotation unless you have cut some words from the end of the final sentence quoted.

21h. The slash

Use the slash to separate two or three lines of poetry that have been run in with your text. Add a space both before and after the slash.

> In the opening lines of "Jordan," George Herbert pokes gentle fun at popular poems of his time: "Who says that fictions only and false hair / Become a verse? Is there in truth no beauty?"

Use the slash sparingly, if at all, to separate options: *pass/fail, producer/director*. Put no space around the slash. Avoid using a slash for *he/she, and/or,* and *his/her*.

Mechanics

22. Capitalization

In addition to the following guidelines, a good dictionary can often tell you when to use capital letters.

22a. Proper versus common nouns

Proper nouns and words derived from them are capitalized; common nouns are not. Proper nouns name specific persons, places, and things. All other nouns are common nouns.

The following types of words are usually capitalized: names for the deity, religions, religious followers, sacred books; words of family relationships used as names; particular places; nationalities and their languages, races, tribes; educational institutions, departments, degrees, particular courses; government departments, organizations, political parties; and historical movements, periods, events, documents.

PROPER NOUNS	COMMON NOUNS
God (used as a name)	a god
Book of Jeremiah	a book
Grandmother Bishop	my grandmother
Father (used as a name)	my father
Lake Superior	a picturesque lake
the Capital Center	a center for advanced studies
the South	a southern state
Japan, a Japanese garden	an ornamental garden
University of Wisconsin	a good university
Veterans Administration	a federal agency
Phi Kappa Psi	a fraternity
a Democrat	an independent
the Enlightenment	the eighteenth century
the Declaration of Independence	a treaty

Months, holidays, and days of the week are capitalized: *May, Labor Day, Monday*. The seasons and numbers of the days of the month are not: *summer, the fifth of June*.

Names of school subjects are capitalized only if they are names of languages: *geology, history, English, French*. Names of particular courses are capitalized: *Geology 101, Principles of Economics*.

CAUTION: Do not capitalize common nouns to make them seem important: *Our company is currently hiring technical support staff* [not *Company, Technical Support Staff*].

22b. Titles with proper names

Capitalize titles of persons when used as part of a proper name but usually not when used alone.

> Prof. Margaret Burnes; Dr. Harold Stevens; John Scott Williams, Jr.; Anne Tilton, LL.D.

> District Attorney Mill was ruled out of order.

> The district attorney was elected for a two-year term.

Usage varies when the title of an important public figure is used alone: *The president* [or *President*] *vetoed the bill.*

22c. Titles of works

In both titles and subtitles of works such as books, articles, and songs, major words should be capitalized. Minor words — articles, prepositions, and coordinating conjunctions — are not capitalized unless they are the first or last word of a title or subtitle. Capitalize the second part of a hyphenated term in a title only if it is a major word.

> *The Country of the Pointed Firs*

> "A Valediction: Of Weeping"

> *The F-Plan Diet*

22d. First word of a sentence or quoted sentence

The first word of a sentence should of course be capitalized. When quoting a sentence, capitalize the first word unless it is blended into the sentence that introduces it.

> In *Time* magazine Robert Hughes writes, "There are only about sixty Watteau paintings on whose authenticity all experts agree."

> Russell Baker has written that in our country "it is sport that is the opiate of the masses."

If a quoted sentence is interrupted by explanatory words, do not capitalize the first word after the interruption.

> "If you wanted to go out," he said sharply, "you should have told me."

22e. First word following a colon

Do not capitalize the first word after a colon unless it begins an independent clause, in which case capitalization is optional.

> Most of the bar's patrons can be divided into two groups: the occasional after-work socializers and the regulars.

> This we are forced to conclude: The [*or* the] federal government is needed to protect the rights of minorities.

22f. Abbreviations

Capitalize abbreviations for departments and agencies of government, other organizations, and corporations; capitalize trade names and the call letters of radio and television stations.

> EPA, FBI, OPEC, IBM, Xerox, WCRB, KNBC-TV

23. Abbreviations, numbers, and italics (underlining)

23a. Abbreviations

Use abbreviations only when they are clearly appropriate.

Appropriate abbreviations. Feel free to use standard abbreviations for titles immediately before and after proper names.

TITLES BEFORE PROPER NAMES	TITLES AFTER PROPER NAMES
Mr. Ralph Meyer	Thomas Hines, Jr.
Ms. Nancy Linehan	Anita Lor, Ph.D.
Dr. Margaret Simmons	Robert Simkowski, M.D.

TITLES BEFORE PROPER NAMES	TITLES AFTER PROPER NAMES
Rev. John Stone	William Lyons, M.A.
St. Joan of Arc	Margaret Chin, LL.D.
Prof. James Russo	Polly Stern, D.D.S.

Do not abbreviate a title if it is not used with a proper name: *My history professor* [not *prof.*] *was an expert on naval warfare.*

Familiar abbreviations for the names of organizations, corporations, and countries are also acceptable.

CIA, FBI, AFL-CIO, NAACP, IBM, UPI, CBS, USA (or U.S.A.)

The YMCA has opened a new gym close to my office.

When using an unfamiliar abbreviation (such as CBE for Council of Biology Editors) throughout a paper, write the full name followed by the abbreviation in parentheses at the first mention of the name. You may use the abbreviation alone from then on.

Other commonly accepted abbreviations include B.C., A.D., A.M., P.M., No., and $. The abbreviation B.C. ("before Christ") follows a date, and A.D. ("*anno Domini*") precedes a date. Acceptable alternatives are B.C.E. ("before the common era") and C.E. ("common era").

40 B.C. (or B.C.E.)	4:00 A.M. (or a.m.)	No. 12 (or no. 12)
A.D. 44 (or C.E.)	6:00 P.M. (or p.m.)	$150

Do not use these abbreviations, however, when they are not accompanied by a specific figure: *We set off for the lake early in the morning* [not *A.M.*].

Inappropriate abbreviations. In formal writing, abbreviations for the following are not commonly accepted.

PERSONAL NAME Charles [*not* Chas.]

UNITS OF MEASUREMENT pound [*not* lb.]

DAYS OF THE WEEK Monday [*not* Mon.]

HOLIDAYS Christmas [*not* Xmas]

MONTHS January, February, March [*not* Jan., Feb., Mar.]

COURSES OF STUDY   political science [*not* poli. sci.]

DIVISIONS OF WRITTEN WORKS   chapter, page [*not* ch., p.]

STATES AND COUNTRIES   Massachusetts [*not* MA or Mass.]

PARTS OF A BUSINESS NAME   Adams Lighting Company [*not* Adams Lighting Co.]; Kim and Brothers, Inc. [*not* Kim and Bros., Inc.]

Although Latin abbreviations are appropriate in footnotes and bibliographies and in informal writing, use the appropriate English phrases in formal writing.

cf. (Latin *confer,* "compare")
e.g. (Latin *exempli gratia,* "for example")
et al. (Latin *et alii,* "and others")
etc. (Latin *et cetera,* "and so forth")
i.e. (Latin *id est,* "that is")
N.B. (Latin *nota bene,* "note well")

23b. Numbers

Spell out numbers of one or two words. Use figures for numbers that require more than two words to spell out.

▶   Now, some ~~8~~ *eight* years later, Muffin is still with us.

▶   Catherine counted ~~one hundred seventy-six~~ *176*

records on the shelf.

EXCEPTION: In technical and some business writing, figures are preferred even when spellings would be brief, but usage varies.

If a sentence begins with a number, spell out the number or rewrite the sentence.

▶   ~~150~~ *One hundred fifty* children in our program need expensive

dental treatment.

Generally, figures are acceptable for the following.

DATES   July 4, 1776, 56 B.C., A.D. 30

ADDRESSES   77 Latches Lane, 519 West 42nd Street

PERCENTAGES   55 percent (or 55%)

FRACTIONS, DECIMALS   ½, 0.047

SCORES   7 to 3, 21–18

STATISTICS   average age 37

SURVEYS   4 out of 5

EXACT AMOUNTS OF MONEY $105.37, $0.05

DIVISIONS OF BOOKS   volume 3, chapter 4, page 189

DIVISIONS OF PLAYS   Act I, scene i (or Act 1, scene 1)

IDENTIFICATION NUMBERS   serial no. 1098

TIME OF DAY   4:00 P.M., 1:30 A.M.

23c. Italics (underlining)

In handwritten or typed papers, <u>underlining</u> represents *italics,* a slanting typeface used in printed material.

Titles of works.   Titles of the following works are italicized or underlined.

TITLES OF BOOKS   *The Great Gatsby, A Distant Mirror*

MAGAZINES   *Time, Scientific American*

NEWSPAPERS   the *St. Louis Post-Dispatch*

PAMPHLETS   *Common Sense, Facts about Marijuana*

LONG POEMS   *The Waste Land, Paradise Lost*

PLAYS   *King Lear, A Raisin in the Sun*

FILMS   *Pulp Fiction, Waiting to Exhale*

TELEVISION PROGRAMS   *Friends, 60 Minutes*

RADIO PROGRAMS   *All Things Considered*

MUSICAL COMPOSITIONS   Gershwin's *Porgy and Bess*

CHOREOGRAPHIC WORKS   Twyla Tharp's *Brief Fling*

WORKS OF VISUAL ART   Rodin's *The Thinker*

COMIC STRIPS   *Dilbert*

SOFTWARE   *WordPerfect*

The titles of other works, such as short stories, essays, songs, and short poems, are enclosed in quotation marks. (See p. 66.)

NOTE: Do not italicize or underline the Bible or the titles of books in the Bible (Genesis, not *Genesis*); the titles of legal documents (the Constitution, not *Constitution*); or the titles of your own papers.

Names of ships, trains, aircraft, spacecraft. Italicize or underline names of specific ships, trains, aircraft, and spacecraft to indicate italics.

> *Challenger, Spirit of St. Louis, Queen Elizabeth II, Silver Streak*

▶ The success of the Soviet's <u>Sputnik</u> galvanized the U.S. space program.

Foreign words. Italicize or underline foreign words used in an English sentence.

▶ Although Joe's method seemed to be successful, I decided to establish my own <u>modus operandi</u>.

EXCEPTION: Do not italicize or underline foreign words that have become part of the English language — "laissez-faire," "fait accompli," "habeas corpus," and "per diem," for example.

Words as words, etc. Italicize or underline words used as words, letters mentioned as letters, and numbers mentioned as numbers.

▶ Tim assured us that the howling probably came from his bloodhound, Billy, but his <u>probably</u> stuck in our minds.

▶ Sarah called her father by his given name, Johnny, but she was unable to pronounce the <u>J</u>.

▶ A big <u>3</u> was painted on the door.

NOTE: Quotation marks may be used instead of italics or underlining to set off words mentioned as words. (See p. 66.)

Inappropriate underlining. Underlining to emphasize words or ideas is distracting and should be used
sparingly.

► Tennis is a sport that has become an ~~addiction.~~

24. Spelling and the hyphen

24a. Spelling

You learned to spell from repeated experience with
words in both reading and writing. Words have a look,
a sound, and even a feel to them as the hand moves
across the page. As you proofread, you can probably
tell if a word doesn't look quite right. In such cases, the
solution is obvious: Look the word up in the dictionary.

A word processor equipped with a spell checker is
a useful alternative to a dictionary, but only up to a
point. A spelling checker will not tell you how to spell
words not listed in its dictionary; nor will it help you
catch words commonly confused, such as *accept* and
except, or common typographical errors, such as *own*
for *won.* You will still need to proofread, and for some
words you may need to turn to the dictionary.

NOTE: To check for correct use of commonly confused
words (*accept* and *except, its* and *it's,* and so on), consult section 34, the Glossary of Usage.

Major spelling rules. If you need to improve your
spelling, review the following rules and exceptions.

1. Use *i* before *e* except after *c* or when sounded
like "ay," as in *neighbor* and *weigh.*

I BEFORE *E*	relieve, believe, sieve, niece, fierce, frieze
E BEFORE *I*	receive, deceive, sleigh, freight, eight
EXCEPTIONS	seize, either, weird, height, foreign, leisure

2. Generally, drop a final silent *e* when adding a
suffix that begins with a vowel. Keep the final *e* if the
suffix begins with a consonant.

desire, desiring	achieve, achievement
remove, removable	care, careful

Words such as *changeable, judgment, argument,* and *truly* are exceptions.

3. When adding -*s* or -*ed* to words ending in -*y,* ordinarily change *y* to *i* when the *y* is preceded by a consonant but not when it is preceded by a vowel.

comedy, comedies	monkey, monkeys
dry, dried	play, played

With proper names ending in -*y,* however, do not change the *y* to *i* even if it is preceded by a consonant: *the Dougherty family, the Doughertys.*

4. If a final consonant is preceded by a single vowel *and* the consonant ends a one-syllable word or a stressed syllable, double the consonant when adding a suffix beginning with a vowel.

bet, betting	occur, occurrence
commit, committed	

5. Add -*s* to form the plural of most nouns; add -*es* to singular nouns ending in -*s, -sh, -ch,* and -*x.*

table, tables	church, churches
paper, papers	dish, dishes

Ordinarily add -*s* to nouns ending in -*o* when the *o* is preceded by a vowel. Add -*es* when it is preceded by a consonant.

radio, radios	hero, heroes
video, videos	tomato, tomatoes

To form the plural of a hyphenated compound word, add the -*s* to the chief word even if it does not appear at the end.

mother-in-law, mothers-in-law

NOTE: English words derived from other languages such as Latin or French sometimes form the plural as they would in their original language.

medium, media	chateau, chateaux
criterion, criteria	

ESL NOTE: Spelling may vary slightly among English-speaking countries. This can prove particularly confusing for ESL students, who may have learned British or Canadian English. Following is a list of some common words spelled differently in American and British English. Consult a dictionary for others.

AMERICAN	BRITISH
canceled, traveled	cancelled, travelled
color, humor	colour, humour
judgment	judgement
check	cheque
realize, apologize	realise, apologise
defense	defence
anemia, anesthetic	anaemia, anaesthetic
theater, center	theatre, centre
fetus	foetus
mold, smolder	mould, smoulder
civilization	civilisation
connection, inflection	connexion, inflexion
licorice	liquorice

Commonly misspelled words. One way to improve your spelling is to work with words that are commonly misspelled. Ask a friend to dictate the following words to you, make a list of any words you misspell, and then practice writing these words correctly.

absence	athlete	conceivable
academic	athletics	conferred
accidentally	attendance	conscience
accommodate	audience	conscious
acknowledge	basically	courteous
acquaintance	beginning	criticism
acquire	believe	curiosity
across	benefited	dealt
address	bureau	decision
all right	business	definitely
altogether	calendar	describe
amateur	candidate	description
analyze	cemetery	desperate
answer	changeable	develop
apparently	characteristic	disappear
appearance	column	disappoint
appropriate	commitment	disastrous
argument	committed	dissatisfied
arrangement	committee	eighth
ascend	competitive	eligible

embarrass
eminent
emphasize
entirely
environment
especially
exaggerated
exhaust
existence
familiar
fascinate
February
foreign
forty
fourth
government
grammar
guidance
harass
height
illiterate
incidentally
incredible
indispensable
inevitable
intelligence
interesting
irrelevant
irresistible
knowledge
laboratory
license

maneuver
mathematics
mischievous
necessary
noticeable
occasionally
occurred
occurrence
omitted
optimistic
pamphlet
parallel
particularly
pastime
perseverance
perspiration
phenomenon
physically
playwright
politics
practically
precede
precedence
preference
preferred
prejudice
privilege
proceed
professor
pronunciation
quiet
quite

recommend
reference
referred
repetition
restaurant
rhythm
ridiculous
roommate
sandwich
schedule
secretary
seize
separate
sergeant
similar
sincerely
sophomore
subtly
succeed
surprise
thorough
tragedy
transferred
truly
unnecessarily
usually
vacuum
vengeance
villain
weird
whether
writing

24b. The hyphen

In addition to the following guidelines, a dictionary will help you make decisions about hyphenation.

Compound words. The dictionary will tell whether to treat a compound word as a hyphenated compound (*water-repellent*), one word (*waterproof*), or two words (*water table*). If the compound word is not in the dictionary, treat it as two words.

▶ The prosecutor chose not to cross^examine any

witnesses.

▶ Nana kept a small note^book in her apron pocket.

▶ Alice walked through the looking/glass into a

   backward world.

Words functioning together as an adjective. When two or more words function together as an adjective before a noun, connect them with a hyphen. Generally, do not use a hyphen when such compounds follow the noun.

▶ Pat Hobbs is not yet a well-known candidate.

▶ After our television campaign, Pat Hobbs will be

   well/known.

Do not use a hyphen to connect *-ly* adverbs to the words they modify.

▶ A slowly/moving truck tied up traffic.

NOTE: In a series, hyphens are suspended: *Do you prefer first-, second-, or third-class tickets?*

Conventional uses. Hyphenate the written form of fractions and of compound numbers from twenty-one to ninety-nine. Also use the hyphen with the prefixes *all-*, *ex-*, and *self-* and with the suffix *-elect*.

▶ One-fourth of my income goes for rent.

▶ The charity is funding more self-help projects.

Division of a word at the end of a line. If a word must be divided at the end of a line, use these guidelines:

1. Divide words between syllables.
2. Never divide one-syllable words.
3. Never divide a word so that a single letter stands alone at the end of a line or fewer than three letters begin a line.
4. When dividing a compound word at the end of a line, either make the break between the words that form the compound or put the whole word on the next line.

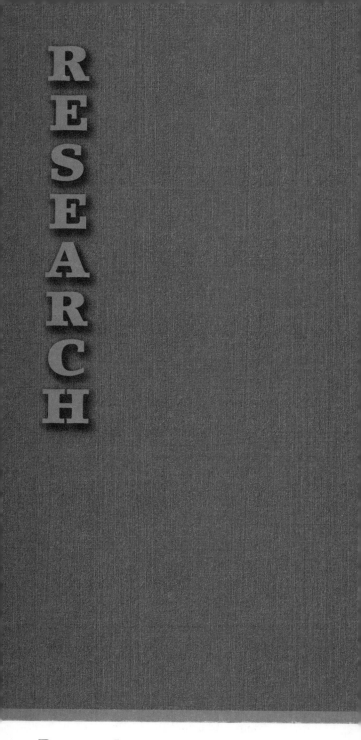

RESEARCH

Researched Writing

In the academic world, writing is often based on reading (and sometimes on field research). This writing may or may not be a full-fledged research paper that draws on a wide variety of sources. Many assignments across the curriculum ask for a response to one, two, or just a few readings.

When doing researched writing, you face three main challenges: (1) supporting a thesis, (2) citing sources and avoiding plagiarism, and (3) integrating quotations and other source material.

25. Supporting a thesis

Most college assignments ask you to form a thesis, or main idea, and to support that thesis with organized and well-documented evidence. Discovering and supporting a thesis is rarely a neat and tidy process — because our first thoughts are not necessarily our wisest thoughts. The more challenging your subject, the more likely you will find yourself adjusting your early thoughts as you read and then write.

25a. Finding a thesis

A thesis is a one-sentence (or occasionally two-sentence) statement of your central idea. Usually your thesis will appear in your opening paragraph, often at its end (see p. 153 for an example). Sometimes the thesis will appear in the second paragraph (see p. 120 for an example). By placing the thesis early in the paper, you tell readers what to expect as they read on.

Although it comes early in your paper, do not attempt to write the thesis until fairly late in your reading and writing process. Reading and rereading will sharpen your ideas. And writing about a subject is a way of learning about it; as you write, your understanding of your subject will almost certainly deepen. As writer E. M. Forster once put it, "How can I know what I think till I see what I say?"

Early in the reading and writing process, you can keep your mind open — yet focused — by posing questions. The thesis that you articulate later in the process will be an answer to the central question you pose.

Here are examples from two disciplines, history and literature.

QUESTION

To what extent was Confederate Major General Nathan Bedford Forrest responsible for the massacre of Union troops at Fort Pillow?

POSSIBLE THESIS

Although we will never know whether Nathan Bedford Forrest directly ordered the massacre of Union troops at Fort Pillow, evidence strongly suggests that he was responsible for it.

QUESTION

In the classical Greek tragedy *Medea*, by Euripides, what is the central conflict: Is it within Medea's own heart (Should I kill my beloved children?) or is it between Medea and Jason, the man who has wronged her (How can I get revenge?)?

POSSIBLE THESIS

Medea professes great love for her children and seems torn between killing them and letting them live, but Euripides gives us reason to suspect her sincerity: Medea does not hesitate to use her children as weapons in her bloody battle with Jason, and from the outset she displays little real concern for their fate.

Notice that both thesis statements take a stand on a debatable issue — an issue about which intelligent, well-meaning people might disagree. Each writer's job will be to convince such people that his or her view is worth taking seriously.

25b. Organizing your evidence

The body of your paper will consist of evidence in support of your thesis. Instead of getting tangled up in details, organize this evidence in bold chunks — maybe three, four, or five chunks, each of which may turn out to be more than one paragraph long in your paper. In other words, keep your plan simple.

Perhaps the most common planning strategy is simply to list the key points in support of your thesis, as this student in a literature class has done:

Medea professes great love for her children and seems torn between killing them and letting them live, but Euripides gives us reason to suspect her sincerity: Medea does not hesitate to use her children as weapons in her bloody battle with Jason, and from the outset she displays little real concern for their fate.

> —From the very beginning of the play, Medea is a less than ideal mother.
> —In three scenes Medea appears to be a loving mother, but in each of these scenes we have reason to doubt her sincerity.
> —Throughout the play, Medea's overriding concern is not her children but her reputation, her fear of ridicule, and her fame.
> —After she kills the children, Medea shows no remorse and revels in Jason's agony over their death.

In the paper itself, this student was careful to begin each chunk of text with a topic sentence focusing the reader's attention on the topic about to be discussed. This was not difficult because she had already drafted such sentences when listing the key points of her paper.

Another common planning strategy is to list specific research questions under the central research question. The specific questions can become a blueprint for the paper, as they did for one student in a history class:

> To what extent was Confederate Major General Nathan Bedford Forrest responsible for the massacre of Union troops at Fort Pillow?
> —What happened at Fort Pillow?
> —Why do the killings qualify as a massacre?
> —Did Forrest order the massacre?
> —Did the men have good reason to think that Forrest wanted a massacre?

To make the organization of his paper clear to readers, this history student used these questions as headings, a technique often used in academic journals. He centered each heading over the chunk of text that it introduced. An example of this technique appears on page 135.

25c. Supporting each point

The key points in your paper should all support your thesis. And each point should in turn be supported by specific, well-documented evidence.

Consider, for example, one of the key points that appeared in the planning materials of the literature student mentioned earlier:

> Throughout the play, Medea's overriding concern is not her children but her reputation, her fear of ridicule, and her fame.

This key point has three parts, each of which became a paragraph in the paper. Here is the second of those paragraphs. Notice that the writer has been careful to document all quotations from the play with line numbers.

> A woman rejected by the man she loves, Medea is highly sensitive to ridicule. She fears that unless she is hard-boiled enough to commit the most hideous of crimes in vengeance for Jason's rejection, people will laugh at her. Early in the play she worries that if she should die in the course of her revenge plot, she would give her enemies "cause for laughter" (383). A bit later she tells herself, "Never / Shall you be mocked by Jason's Corinthian wedding, / Whose father was noble, whose grandfather Helius" (404–06). Her first justification of her plan for killing the children is that it would not be bearable to be "mocked by enemies" (797). Later, when Medea debates whether to kill the children, she asks herself, "Do I want to let go / My enemies unhurt and be laughed at for it? I must face this thing" (1049–51). Finally, facing Jason after she has killed the children, Medea proclaims, "No, it was not to be that you should scorn my love, / And pleasantly live your life through laughing at me" (1354–55).

Although the examples in this paragraph are given in chronological order, the student is not simply summarizing the plot. Instead, she uses examples from the text of the play to support an interpretation: that Medea, as portrayed by Euripides, is indeed highly sensitive to ridicule.

26. When to cite a source; avoiding plagiarism

In researched writing, you will be drawing on the work of other writers, and you must document their contributions by citing your sources. Sources are cited for two reasons: to tell readers where your information comes from and to give credit to the writers from whom you have borrowed words and ideas. To borrow another writer's language or ideas without proper acknowledgment is a form of dishonesty known as plagiarism.

26a. Using a consistent system for citing sources

Citations are required when you quote from a source, when you summarize or paraphrase a source, and when you borrow facts and ideas from a source (except for common knowledge). (See also 26b.)

The various academic disciplines use their own editorial styles for citing sources. Most English instructors prefer the Modern Language Association's system of in-text citations. Here, very briefly, is how an MLA in-text citation usually works:

1. The source is introduced by a signal phrase that names its author.
2. The quoted words or borrowed ideas are followed by a page number in parentheses.
3. At the end of the paper, a list of works cited (arranged alphabetically according to the authors' last names) gives complete publishing information about the source.

SAMPLE IN-TEXT CITATION

According to Eugene Linden, some psychologists have adopted the oddly unscientific attitude that "the idea of the language capacity of apes is so preposterous that it should not be investigated at all" (11).

SAMPLE ENTRY IN THE LIST OF WORKS CITED

```
Linden, Eugene. Silent Partners: The Legacy of
     the Ape Language Experiments. New York:
     Times, 1986.
```

Handling an MLA citation is not always so simple. When the author is not named in a signal phrase, for example, the parentheses must include the author's last name along with the page number. For a detailed discussion of this and other variations, see 29.

If your instructor has asked you to use the APA style of in-text citation, consult 31; if your instructor prefers footnotes or endnotes, consult 32. For a list of style manuals used in a variety of disciplines, see 33.

26b. Avoiding plagiarism

Your research paper is a collaboration between you and your sources. To be fair and ethical, you must acknowledge your debt to the writers of these sources. If you don't, you are guilty of plagiarism, a serious academic offense.

Three different acts are considered plagiarism: (1) failing to cite quotations and borrowed ideas, (2) failing to enclose borrowed language in quotation marks, and (3) failing to put summaries and paraphrases in your own words.

Citing quotations and borrowed ideas. You must of course cite the source of all direct quotations. You must also cite any ideas borrowed from a source: paraphrases of sentences, summaries of paragraphs or chapters, statistics and little-known facts, and tables, graphs, or diagrams.

The only exception is common knowledge — information that your readers could find in any number of general sources because it is commonly known. For example, the current population of the United States is common knowledge in such fields as sociology and economics; Freud's theory of the unconscious is common knowledge in the field of psychology.

As a rule, when you have seen certain information repeatedly in your reading, you don't need to cite it. However, when information has appeared in only one or two sources or when it is controversial, you should cite it. If a topic is new to you and you are not sure what is considered common knowledge or what is a matter of controversy, ask someone with expertise. When in doubt, cite the source.

NOTE: The examples in 26–28 use MLA-style citations (see 29).

Enclosing borrowed language in quotation marks. To indicate that you are using a source's exact phrases or sentences, you must enclose them in quotation marks unless they have been set off from the text by indenting. (See 27c.) To omit the quotation marks is to claim — falsely — that the language is your own. Such an omission is plagiarism even if you have cited the source.

ORIGINAL SOURCE

No animal has done more to renew interest in animal intelligence than a beguiling, bilingual bonobo named Kanzi, who has the grammatical abilities of a 2½-year-old child and a taste for movies about cavemen.
— Eugene Linden, "Animals," p. 57

PLAGIARISM

According to Eugene Linden, no animal has done more to renew interest in animal intelligence than a beguiling, bilingual bonobo named Kanzi, who has the grammatical abilities of a 2-1/2-year-old child and a taste for movies about cavemen (57).

BORROWED LANGUAGE IN QUOTATION MARKS

According to Eugene Linden, "No animal has done more to renew interest in animal intelligence than a beguiling, bilingual bonobo named Kanzi, who has the grammatical abilities of a 2-1/2-year-old child and a taste for movies about cavemen" (57).

Putting summaries and paraphrases in your own words. When you summarize or paraphrase, it is not enough to name the source; you must restate the source's meaning using your own language. You are guilty of plagiarism if you half-copy the author's sentences — either by mixing the author's well-chosen phrases without using quotation marks or by plugging your own synonyms into the author's sentence structure. The following paraphrases are plagiarized — even though the source is cited — because their language is too close to that of the source.

ORIGINAL SOURCE

If the existence of a signing ape was unsettling for linguists, it was also startling news for animal behaviorists.   —Davis, *Eloquent Animals*, p. 26

UNACCEPTABLE BORROWING OF PHRASES

The existence of a signing ape unsettled linguists and startled animal behaviorists (Davis 26).

UNACCEPTABLE BORROWING OF STRUCTURE

If the presence of a sign-language-using chimp was disturbing for scientists studying language, it was also surprising to scientists studying animal behavior (Davis 26).

To avoid plagiarizing an author's language, resist the temptation to look at the source while you are summarizing or paraphrasing. Close the book, write from memory, and then open the book to check for accuracy. This technique prevents you from being captivated by the words on the page.

ACCEPTABLE PARAPHRASES

When they learned of an ape's ability to use sign language, both linguists and animal behaviorists were taken by surprise (Davis 26).

According to Flora Davis, linguists and animal behaviorists were unprepared for the news that

a chimp could communicate with its trainers
through sign language (26).

27. How to integrate quotations

Readers should be able to move from your own words
to the words you quote from a source without feeling
a jolt.

27a. Using signal phrases

Avoid dropping quotations into the text without warning; instead, provide clear signal phrases, usually including the author's name, to prepare readers for the
source.

DROPPED QUOTATION

Perhaps even more significant is the pattern that
Kanzi developed on his own in combining various
lexigrams. "When he gave an order combining two
symbols for action--such as 'chase' and 'hide'--
it was important for him that the first action--
'chase'--be done first" (Gibbons 1561).

QUOTATION WITH SIGNAL PHRASE

Perhaps even more significant is the pattern
that Kanzi developed on his own in combining
various lexigrams. According to Ann Gibbons,
"When he gave an order combining two symbols
for action--such as 'chase' and 'hide'--it was
important for him that the first action--
'chase'--be done first" (1561).

To avoid monotony, try to vary your signal phrases.
The following models suggest a range of possibilities.

In the words of researcher Herbert Terrace, "..."

As Flora Davis has noted, "..."

The Gardners, Washoe's trainers, point out that "..."

". . .," claims linguist Noam Chomsky.

". . .," writes Erik Eckholm, ". . ."

Psychologist H. S. Terrace offers an odd argument for this view: ". . ."

Terrace answers these objections with the following analysis: ". . ."

When the signal phrase includes a verb, choose one that is appropriate in the context. Is your source arguing a point, making an observation, reporting a fact, drawing a conclusion, refuting an argument, or stating a belief? By choosing an appropriate verb, such as one on the following list, you can make your source's stance clear.

admits	contends	reasons
agrees	declares	refutes
argues	denies	rejects
asserts	emphasizes	reports
believes	insists	responds
claims	notes	suggests
compares	observes	thinks
confirms	points out	writes

It is not always necessary to quote full sentences from a source. At times you may wish to borrow only a phrase or to weave part of a source's sentence into your own sentence structure.

```
Bruce Bower reports that Kanzi practices "simple
grammatical ordering rules," such as putting
actions before objects (140).
```

```
Perhaps the best summation of the current state of
ape language studies comes from biologist Robert
Seyfarth, who writes that the line separating
humans from other animals "remains hazily drawn,
somewhere between the word and the sentence" (18).
```

27b. Using the ellipsis mark and brackets

Two useful marks of punctuation, the ellipsis mark and brackets, allow you to keep quoted material to a minimum and to integrate it smoothly into your own text.

The ellipsis mark.   To condense a quoted passage, you can use the ellipsis mark (three periods, with spaces between) to indicate that you have omitted words. The sentence that remains must be grammatically complete.

```
Erik Eckholm reports that "a 4-year-old pygmy

chimpanzee . . . has demonstrated what scien-

tists say are the most humanlike linguistic

skills ever documented in another animal" (A1).
```

The writer has omitted the words *at a research center near Atlanta*, which appeared in the original.

When you want to omit a full sentence or more, use a period before the three ellipsis dots.

```
According to Wade, the horse Clever Hans "could

apparently count by tapping out numbers with

his hoof. . . . Clever Hans owes his celebrity

to his master's innocence. Von Osten sincerely

believed he had taught Hans to solve arithmeti-

cal problems" (1349).
```

Ordinarily, do not use an ellipsis mark at the beginning or at the end of a quotation. Readers will understand that the quoted material is taken from a longer passage. The only exception occurs when you have omitted words at the end of the final quoted sentence.

Brackets.   Brackets allow you to insert words of your own into quoted material, perhaps to explain a confusing reference or to keep a sentence grammatical in your context.

```
Robert Seyfarth writes that "Premack [a scientist

at the University of Pennsylvania] taught a

seven-year-old chimpanzee, Sarah, that the word

for 'apple' was a small, plastic triangle" (13).
```

If you are working on a typewriter that has no brackets, ink them in by hand.

27c. Setting off long quotations

When you quote more than four typed lines of prose or more than three lines of poetry, set off the quotation by indenting it one inch (or ten spaces) from the left margin. Use the normal right margin and do not single-space.

Long quotations should be introduced by an informative sentence, usually followed by a colon. Quotation marks are unnecessary because the indented format tells readers that the words are taken directly from the source.

```
Desmond describes how Washoe, when the Gardners
returned her to an ape colony in Oklahoma, tried
signing to the other apes:
            One particularly memorable day, a
        snake spread terror through the
        castaways on the ape island, and all
        but one fled in panic. This male sat
        absorbed, staring intently at the
        serpent. Then Washoe was seen running
        over signing to him "come, hurry up."
        (42)
```

Notice that in MLA style, the parenthetical citation at the end of an indented quotation goes outside the final period.

NOTE: APA guidelines for setting off long quotations are slightly different. See page 131.

27d. Quoting a source quoted in another source

Occasionally you may want to quote a source that was quoted in a book or article you consulted. You can do this, but make sure that you integrate the quotation into your text with your own signal phrase. Do not borrow the signal phrase used by the author of the book or article you consulted.

SOURCE YOU CONSULTED

Terrace has his backers. According to linguist, semanticist and anthropologist Thomas A. Sebeok
of the University of Indiana, ape-language researchers fall into "three categories: self-delusional
and self-deceptive, fraudulent, and Herb Terrace
. . . we agree wholeheartedly."
— Joel Greenberg, "Ape Talk: More
Than 'Pigeon' English?," p. 229

YOUR OWN SIGNAL PHRASE

One of the harshest critics of the ape language
studies, Thomas A. Sebeok, sarcastically dis-
misses all researchers except Herbert Terrace by
placing the researchers into three categories:
"self-delusional and self-deceptive, fraudulent,
and Herb Terrace . . . we agree wholeheartedly"
(qtd. in Greenberg 229).

To borrow Joel Greenberg's signal phrase — *According
to linguist, semanticist and anthropologist Thomas A.
Sebeok of the University of Indiana* — would be plagiarism. (See 26b.)

28. How to integrate other source material

Besides quotations, your source material may include
(1) summaries and paraphrases and (2) statistics and
other facts.

28a. Integrating summaries and paraphrases

Introduce most summaries and paraphrases with a signal phrase that names the author and places the material in context. Readers will then understand that
everything between the signal phrase and the parenthetical citation summarizes or paraphrases the cited
source.

Without the signal phrase (underlined) in the following example, readers might think that only the last sentence is being cited, when in fact the whole paragraph is based on the source.

> Recent studies at the Yerkes Primate Center in Atlanta are breaking new ground. <u>Researchers Patricia Greenfield and Sue Savage-Rumbaugh report that</u> the pygmy chimp Kanzi seems to understand simple grammatical rules about lexigram order. For instance, Kanzi learned that in two-word utterances action precedes object, an ordering also used by human children at the two-word stage. What is impressive, say Greenfield and Savage-Rumbaugh, is that in addition to being semantically related, most of Kanzi's lexigram combinations are original (556).

There are times, however, when a signal phrase naming the author is not necessary. Most readers will understand, for example, that the citation at the end of the following passage applies to the entire anecdote, not just the last sentence.

> One afternoon, Koko the gorilla, who was often bored with language lessons, stubbornly and repeatedly signaled "red" in American Sign Language when asked the color of a white towel. She did this even though she had correctly identified the color white many times before. At last the gorilla plucked a bit of red lint from the towel and showed it to her trainer (Patterson and Linden 80-81).

Notice that when there is no signal phrase naming the author, the authors' names must be included in the parentheses along with the page number.

28b. Integrating statistics and other facts

When you are citing a statistic or other specific fact, a signal phrase is often not necessary. In most cases, readers will understand that the citation refers to the statistic or fact (not the whole paragraph).

```
By 1991 Kanzi, a ten-year-old pygmy chimp, had
learned to communicate about two hundred symbols
on the computerized board that he carries with
him (Lewin 51).
```

There is nothing wrong, however, with using a signal phrase.

```
Roger Lewin reports that by 1991 the ten-year-
old pygmy chimp Kanzi had learned to communicate
about two hundred symbols on the computerized
board that he carries with him (51).
```

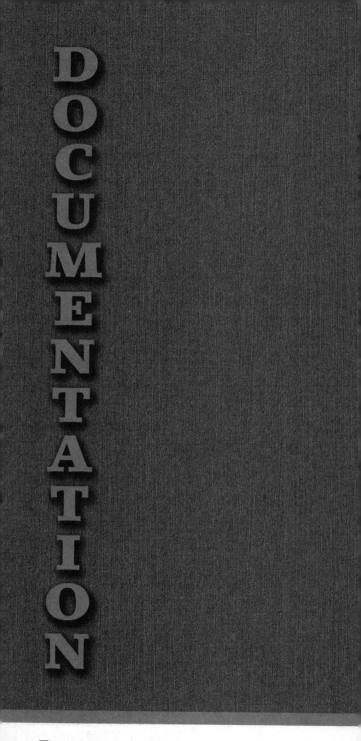

Documentation

In research papers and in any other academic writing that borrows information from sources, the borrowed information must be clearly documented. (See 26 for guidelines on when to cite a source.)

You should use the system of documentation recommended by your instructor. *A Pocket Style Manual* describes three systems: MLA style, used in English and the humanities; APA style, used in the social sciences; and *Chicago* style, also used in the humanities, particularly in history. See sections 29, 31, and 32. For recent guidelines on documenting electronic sources, see 30. For other systems of documentation, consult the list of style manuals in 33.

29. MLA documentation style

To document sources, the Modern Language Association (MLA) recommends in-text citations that refer readers to a list of works cited.

DIRECTORY TO MLA IN-TEXT CITATIONS	
1. Author named in a signal phrase	104
2. Author not named in a signal phrase	104
3. Two or three authors	104
4. Four or more authors	104
5. Corporate author	105
6. Unknown author	105
7. Two or more works by the same author	105
8. A source quoted in another source	105
9. Work in an anthology	106
10. Novel, play, or poem	106
11. Multivolume source	107
12. Entire work	107
13. Two or more works	107
14. Authors with the same last name	107
15. Work without page numbers	107

29a. MLA in-text citations

An MLA in-text citation is made with a combination of a signal phrase and a parenthetical reference. The signal phrase usually names the author of the source;

the parenthetical reference includes at least a page number.

1. Author named in a signal phrase. By naming the author in a signal phrase, you can keep the information in parentheses brief. Usually only a page number is required.

```
Flora Davis reports that a chimp at the Yerkes
Primate Research Center "has combined words into
new sentences that she was never taught" (67).
```

The signal phrase — *Flora Davis reports* — provides the name of the author; the parenthetical citation gives the page number where the quoted words may be found. By looking up the author's last name in the list of works cited, readers will find complete information about the work's title, publisher, and date of publication.

2. Author not named in a signal phrase. If the signal phrase does not include the author's name (or if there is no signal phrase), the author's last name must appear in parentheses with the page number.

```
Although the baby chimp lived only a few hours,
Washoe signed to it before it died (Davis 42).
```

3. Two or three authors. Name the authors in a signal phrase or include their last names in the parentheses along with the page number: (Patterson and Linden 89).

```
Patterson and Linden agree that the gorilla Koko
acquired language more slowly than a normal
speaking child (89).
```

4. Four or more authors. Name the first author and mention the coauthors in a signal phrase or put the first author's name followed by "et al." (Latin for "and others") in the parentheses: (Terrace et al. 891).

```
Ultimately Terrace and his coauthors concluded
that "most of Nim's utterances were prompted by
his teacher's prior utterance" (891).
```

5. Corporate author. Name the corporate author in a signal phrase or in the parentheses: (Internal Revenue Service 43).

The Internal Revenue Service warns businesses that deductions for "lavish and extravagant entertainment" are not allowed (43).

6. Unknown author. Mention the full title in a signal phrase or use a short form of the title in the parentheses. Titles or short titles of books are underlined or italicized: (*Times Atlas* 43). Titles or short titles of articles are put in quotation marks: ("Black" 103).

According to "Black, Blue, and Gray: The Other Civil War," black Americans, both slave and free, "provided the margin of difference that turned the tide against the Confederate forces in 1864 and 1865" (103).

7. Two or more works by the same author. If your list of works cited contains two or more works by the same author, mention the full title of the work in the signal phrase or use a short form of the title in the parentheses: (*Eloquent* 67).

In Eloquent Animals, Flora Davis reports that a chimp at the Yerkes Primate Research Center "has combined words into sentences that she was never taught" (67).

In the rare case when both the author and a shortened title must be given in parentheses, the citation should appear like this: (Davis, *Eloquent* 67).

8. A source quoted in another source. When a writer's or speaker's quoted words appear in a work written by another author, use the abbreviation "qtd. in" before the author's name in the parentheses.

"We only used seven signs in his presence," says Fouts. "All of his signs were learned from

the other chimps at the laboratory" (qtd. in
Toner 24).

9. Work in an anthology.   Put the name of the author of the work (not the editor of the anthology) in the
signal phrase or in the parentheses: (Chopin 25).

At the end of Kate Chopin's "The Story of an
Hour," Mrs. Mallard drops dead upon learning
that her husband is alive. In the final irony
of the story, doctors report that she has died
of a "joy that kills" (25).

10. Novel, play, or poem.   Include information that
will enable readers to find the passage in various edi-
tions of the work. For a novel, put the page number
first and then, if possible, indicate the part or chapter
in which the passage can be found.

Fitzgerald's narrator captures Gatsby in a
moment of isolation: "A sudden emptiness seemed
to flow now from the windows and the great
doors, endowing with complete isolation the
figure of the host" (56; ch. 3).

For a verse play, list the act, scene, and line numbers.
Use arabic numerals.

In his famous advice to the players, Hamlet
defines the purpose of theater, "whose end, both
at the first and now, was and is, to hold, as
'twere, the mirror up to nature" (3.2.21-23).

For a poem, cite the part (if there are a number of
parts) and the line numbers.

When Homer's Odysseus comes to the hall of
Circe, he finds his men "mild / in her soft
spell, fed on her drug of evil" (10.209-11).

11. *Multivolume source.* If your paper cites more than one volume of a multivolume source, you must indicate in the parentheses which volume you are referring to.

```
Terman's studies of gifted children reveal a
pattern of accelerated language acquisition
(2:279).
```

12. *Entire work.* To cite an entire work, use the author's name in a signal phrase or a parenthetical reference.

```
Patterson and Linden provide convincing evidence
for the speech-making abilities of nonhuman
primates.
```

13. *Two or more works.* You may want to cite more than one source to document a particular point. Separate the citations with a semicolon.

```
With intensive training, the apes in this study
learned more than two hundred signs or signals
(Desmond 229; Linden 173).
```

14. *Authors with the same last name.* If your list of works cited includes works by two or more authors with the same last name, include the first name of the author you are citing in the signal phrase or parenthetical reference.

```
Both Lucy and Koko have been reported to lie
(Adrian Desmond 201).
```

15. *Work without page numbers.* You may omit the page number if a work has no page numbers or if a work is only one page long or is organized alphabetically (as with encyclopedias). Some electronic sources use paragraph numbers instead of page numbers. For such sources use the abbreviation "par." or "pars." in the parentheses: (Smith, par. 4).

29b. MLA list of works cited

An alphabetized list of works cited, which appears at the end of your paper, gives full publishing information for each of the sources you have cited in the paper. For advice on constructing the list and typing it according to MLA guidelines, see page 118. A sample list of works cited appears on page 121.

The following models illustrate the MLA form for entries in the list of works cited.

DIRECTORY TO MLA LIST OF WORKS CITED

BOOKS

1.	Basic format for a book	109
2.	Two or three authors	109
3.	Four or more authors	110
4.	Unknown author	110
5.	Corporate author	110
6.	Editor	110
7.	Author with an editor	110
8.	Translation	110
9.	Two or more works by the same author	110
10.	Edition other than the first	110
11.	Multivolume work	111
12.	Work in an anthology	111
13.	Introduction or preface	111
14.	Unsigned encyclopedia article	111
15.	Book title within a book title	111
16.	Title in quotation marks within a book title	111
17.	Book in a series	111
18.	Republished book	112

PERIODICALS

19.	Article in a monthly magazine	112
20.	Article in a weekly magazine	112
21.	Article in a newspaper	112
22.	Article in a journal paginated by volume	112
23.	Article in a journal paginated by issue	112
24.	Unsigned periodical article	112
25.	Review	112
26.	Editorial	113
27.	Letter to the editor	113

CD-ROMS AND ONLINE SOURCES

28. CD-ROM issued periodically   113
29. CD-ROM issued in a single edition   113
30. Online material from a computer service   113
31. Online material from a computer network   113
32. Online journal   113

OTHER SOURCES

33. Pamphlet or government publication   114
34. Dissertation   114
35. Dissertation abstract   114
36. Personal interview   114
37. Published interview   114
38. Film or videotape   114
39. Radio or television program   115
40. Live performance of a play   115
41. Record, tape, or CD   115
42. Published proceedings of a conference   115
43. Work of art   115
44. Personal letter   115
45. E-mail   115
46. Online posting to a newsgroup   116
47. Lecture or public address   116
48. Cartoon   116
49. Map or chart   116

Books

1. BASIC FORMAT FOR A BOOK

For most books, arrange the information into three units, each followed by a period: (1) the author's name, last name first; (2) the title and subtitle, underlined or italicized; and (3) the place of publication, the publisher, and the date.

McPherson, James M. <u>Battle Cry of Freedom: The</u>

   <u>Civil War Era</u>. New York: Oxford UP, 1988.

2. TWO OR THREE AUTHORS

Bentley, Nicolas, Michael Slater, and Nina

   Burgis. <u>The Dickens Index</u>. New York: Oxford

   UP, 1990.

3. FOUR OR MORE AUTHORS

Medhurst, Martin J., et al. <u>Cold War Rhetoric:</u>
<u>Strategy, Metaphor, and Ideology</u>. New York:
Greenwood, 1990.

4. UNKNOWN AUTHOR

<u>The Times Atlas of the World</u>. 9th ed. New York:
New York Times, 1992.

5. CORPORATE AUTHOR

Fidelity Investments. <u>Mutual Brokerage Services</u>
<u>Handbook</u>. Boston: Fidelity Investments,
1993.

6. EDITOR

Dubus, Andre, ed. <u>Into the Silence: American</u>
<u>Stories</u>. Cambridge: Green Street, 1988.

7. AUTHOR WITH AN EDITOR

Douglass, Frederick. <u>Narrative of the Life of</u>
<u>Frederick Douglass, an American Slave</u>. Ed.
David W. Blight. Boston: Bedford, 1993.

8. TRANSLATION

Eco, Umberto. <u>Foucault's Pendulum</u>. Trans.
William Weaver. San Diego: Harcourt, 1989.

9. TWO OR MORE WORKS BY THE SAME AUTHOR

Brown, Rita Mae. <u>Riding Shotgun</u>. New York:
Bantam, 1996.

---. <u>Rubyfruit Jungle</u>. New York: Bantam, 1988.

10. EDITION OTHER THAN THE FIRST

Wilson, Edwin, and Alvin Goldfarb. <u>Living</u>
<u>Theater: A History</u>. 2nd ed. New York:
McGraw, 1994.

11. MULTIVOLUME WORK

Foote, Shelby. The Civil War: A Narrative.

    3 vols. New York: Random, 1958-74.

12. WORK IN AN ANTHOLOGY

Truong, Bao-Tran. "Stepping Stones in America."

    Where Coyotes Howl and Wind Blows Free:

    Growing Up in the West. Ed. Alexandra R.

    Haslam and Gerald W. Haslam. Reno: U of

    Nevada P, 1995. 152-56.

13. INTRODUCTION OR PREFACE

Van Vechten, Carl. Introduction. Last Operas

    and Plays. By Gertrude Stein. Ed. Van

    Vechten. New York: Vintage-Random, 1975.

    vii-xix.

14. UNSIGNED ENCYCLOPEDIA ARTICLE

"Croatia." The New Encyclopaedia Britannica:

    Micropaedia. 1991.

15. BOOK TITLE WITHIN A BOOK TITLE

Abbott, Keith. Downstream from Trout Fishing in

    America: A Memoir of Richard Brautigan.

    Santa Barbara: Capra, 1989.

16. TITLE IN QUOTATION MARKS WITHIN A BOOK TITLE

Faulkner, Dewey R. Twentieth Century Interpreta-

    tions of "The Pardoner's Tale." Englewood

    Cliffs: Spectrum-Prentice, 1973.

17. BOOK IN A SERIES

Laughlin, Robert M. Of Cabbages and Kings: Tales

    from Zinacantán. Smithsonian Contributions

    to Anthropology 23. Washington: Smithsonian,

    1977.

18. REPUBLISHED BOOK

McClintock, Walter. <u>Old Indian Trails</u>. 1926.

Foreword William Least Heat Moon. Boston:

Houghton, 1992.

Periodicals

19. ARTICLE IN A MONTHLY MAGAZINE

Harrison, Barbara Grizzuti. "Collecting the Stuff

of Life." <u>Harper's</u> May 1996: 15-19.

20. ARTICLE IN A WEEKLY MAGAZINE

Weil, Andrew. "The New Politics of Coca." <u>New

Yorker</u> 15 May 1995: 70-80.

21. ARTICLE IN A NEWSPAPER

Browne, Malcolm W. "Math Experts Say Asteroid May

Hit Earth in Million Years." <u>New York Times</u>

25 Apr. 1996: B10.

22. ARTICLE IN A JOURNAL PAGINATED BY VOLUME

Segal, Gabriel. "Seeing What Is Not There."

<u>Philosophical Review</u> 98 (1989): 189-214.

23. ARTICLE IN A JOURNAL PAGINATED BY ISSUE

Johnson, G. J. "A Distinctiveness Model of

Serial Learning." <u>Psychological Review</u>

98.2 (1991): 204-17.

24. UNSIGNED PERIODICAL ARTICLE

"Covert Operation." <u>National Times</u> Apr. 1996: 51.

25. REVIEW

Shetley, Vernon. "The Changing Light." Rev. of <u>A

Scattering of Salts</u>, by James Merrill. <u>New

Republic</u> 5 June 1995: 38.

26. EDITORIAL

"Limits on Democracy." Editorial. <u>Boston Globe</u>
    23 May 1995: 18.

27. LETTER TO THE EDITOR

Benston, Graham. Letter. <u>Opera Now</u> May 1993: 12.

CD-ROMs and online sources

28. CD-ROM ISSUED PERIODICALLY

Sawyer, Kathy. "Oceanography: Rising Tide Lifts
    Warming Case." <u>Washington Post</u> 12 Dec.
    1994: A2. <u>InfoTrac: National Newspaper</u>
    <u>Index</u>. CD-ROM. Information Access. Jan.
    1995.

29. CD-ROM ISSUED IN A SINGLE EDITION

"O'Keeffe, Georgia." <u>The 1995 Grolier Multimedia</u>
    <u>Encyclopedia</u>. CD-ROM. Danbury: Grolier,
    1995.

30. ONLINE MATERIAL FROM A COMPUTER SERVICE

Mann, Charles C., and Mark L. Plummer. "Empower-
    ing Species." <u>Atlantic Monthly</u> Feb. 1995.
    <u>Atlantic Monthly Online</u>. Online. America
    Online. 16 Feb. 1995.

31. ONLINE MATERIAL FROM A COMPUTER NETWORK

Spetalnick, Terrie. "Privacy in the Electronic
    Community." <u>EDUCOM Review</u> 28.3 (1993): n.
    pag. Online. Internet. 7 Feb. 1995.
    Available: gopher.cic.net.

32. ONLINE JOURNAL

Page, Barbara. "Women Writers and the Restive
    Text: Feminism, Experimental Writing, and

Hypertext." <u>Postmodern Culture</u> 6.2 (1996):
n. pag. Online. Internet. 3 Apr. 1996.
Available: gopher://jefferson.village.
virginia.edu:70/00/pubs/pmc/issue.196/
page.196.

Other sources

33. PAMPHLET OR GOVERNMENT PUBLICATION

United States. Dept. of the Interior. National
Park Service. <u>Ford's Theatre and the
House Where Lincoln Died</u>. Washington: GPO,
1989.

34. DISSERTATION

Fedorko, Kathy Anne. "Edith Wharton's Haunted
House: The Gothic in Her Fiction." Diss.
Rutgers U, 1987.

35. DISSERTATION ABSTRACT

Berkman, Anne Elizabeth. "The Quest for
Authenticity: The Novels of Toni Morrison."
<u>DAI</u> 48 (1988): 2059A. Columbia U.

36. PERSONAL INTERVIEW

Shaw, Lloyd. Personal interview. 21 Mar. 1996.

37. PUBLISHED INTERVIEW

Ehrenreich, Barbara. Interview. <u>Progressive</u>. Feb.
1995: 34-38.

38. FILM OR VIDEOTAPE

<u>North by Northwest</u>. Dir. Alfred Hitchcock. With
Cary Grant and Eva Marie Saint. MGM, 1959.

<u>Through the Wire</u>. Dir. Nina Rosenblum.
Narr. Susan Sarandon. Videocassette.
Fox/Lorber Home Video, 1990.

39. RADIO OR TELEVISION PROGRAM

Be-Bop City. With Michael Anderson. WBGO,

    Newark. 23 May 1995.

"This Old Pyramid." With Mark Lehner and Roger

    Hopkins. Nova. PBS. WGBH, Boston. 4 Aug.

    1993.

40. LIVE PERFORMANCE OF A PLAY

The Sisters Rosensweig. By Wendy Wasserstein.

    Dir. Daniel Sullivan. With Jane Alexander,

    Christine Estabrook, and Madeline Kahn.

    Barrymore, New York. 11 July 1993.

41. RECORD, TAPE, OR CD

Handel, George Frideric. Messiah. Cond. Charles

    Mackerras. English Chamber Orch. and the

    Ambrosian Singers. Angel, R 67-2682, 1967.

42. PUBLISHED PROCEEDINGS OF A CONFERENCE

Howell, Benita J., ed. Cultural Heritage

    Conservation in the American South. Proc.

    of Southern Anthropology Society. Tampa,

    1988. Athens: U of Georgia P, 1990.

43. WORK OF ART

Cassatt, Mary. At the Opera. Museum of Fine

    Arts, Boston.

44. PERSONAL LETTER

Cipriani, Karen. Letter to the author. 25 Apr.

    1996.

45. E-MAIL

Recinto, David. "Accounting Procedures." E-mail

    to Janice Doren. 7 Feb. 1996.

Roth, Rachel. E-mail to the author. 10 May 1996.

46. ONLINE POSTING TO A NEWSGROUP

Ventresca, Lucy. "Winemaking." 20 Jan. 1996. On-

line posting. Newsgroup soc.culture.italian.

Usenet. 1 Feb. 1996.

47. LECTURE OR PUBLIC ADDRESS

Quinn, Karen. "John Singleton Copley's Watson

and the Shark." Museum of Fine Arts,

Boston. 1 July 1993.

48. CARTOON

Chast, Roz. "Are You All Right?" Cartoon. New

Yorker 5 July 1993: 65.

49. MAP OR CHART

Spain/Portugal. Map. Paris: Michelin, 1992.

29c. MLA information notes

Writers who use the MLA system of in-text citations may also use information notes for one of two purposes:

1. to provide additional information that might interrupt the flow of the paper yet is important enough to include;
2. to refer readers to sources not included in the list of works cited.

Information notes may be either footnotes or endnotes. Footnotes appear at the bottom of the page; endnotes appear at the end of the paper, just before the list of works cited. For either style, the notes are numbered consecutively throughout the paper. The text of the paper contains a raised arabic numeral that corresponds to the number of the note.

TEXT

There is still skepticism about whether the apes

merely imitate or respond to the cues of their

trainers.[1]

NOTE

[1] For a discussion of this issue, see Thomas A. Sebeok and Jean Umiker-Sebeok, "Performing Animals: Secrets of the Trade," <u>Psychology Today</u> Nov. 1979: 78-91.

29d. MLA manuscript format

The Modern Language Association makes the following recommendations about manuscript format.

Title and identification. Although MLA does not require a title page, many instructors prefer that you use one. For an example, see page 119.

If you don't use a title page, put the following information, on separate lines, against the left margin about one inch from the top of your first page: your name, the instructor's name, the course name and number, and the date. Double-space between lines. Then double-space again and center the title of the paper in the width of the page. Double-space once more and begin typing the text of the paper.

Margins, spacing, and indentation. Leave margins of at least one inch but no more than an inch and a half on all sides of the page. Do not justify the right margin.

Double-space between lines and indent the first line of each paragraph five spaces (one-half inch) from the left margin.

For quotations longer than four typed lines of prose or three lines of verse, indent each line ten spaces (one inch) from the left margin. Double-space between the body of the paper and the quotation, and double-space the lines of the quotation.

Pagination. Using arabic numerals, number all pages at the upper right corner, one-half inch below the top edge. Put your last name before each page number for clear identification in case pages are misplaced.

Punctuation and typing. In typing the paper, leave one space after words, commas, colons, and semicolons and between dots in ellipsis marks. MLA allows either one or two spaces after periods, question marks, and exclamation points. To form a dash, type two hyphens with no space between them; do not put a space on either side of a dash.

Preparing the "Works Cited" page

On page 121 is a sample list of works cited. The list of works cited appears at the end of the paper.

To construct such a list, begin on a new page and title your list "Works Cited." Alphabetize the list by the last names of the authors (or editors); if a work has no author or editor, alphabetize by the first word of the title other than *A*, *An*, or *The*.

If two or more works by the same author appear in the list, use the author's name only for the first entry. For subsequent entries, use three hyphens followed by a period. List the titles in alphabetical order.

Do not indent the first line of each entry in the list but indent any additional lines five spaces (one-half inch). Double-space throughout.

NOTE: The sample "Works Cited" page shows you how to type the list. For information about the exact format of each entry in the list of works cited, consult the models on pages 109–16.

Between the Word and the Sentence:

Apes and Language

Karen Shaw

English 101, Section 30

Dr. Robert Barshay

4 November 1996

Between the Word and the Sentence:
Apes and Language

One afternoon, Koko the gorilla, who was often bored with language lessons, stubbornly and repeatedly signaled "red" in American Sign Language when asked the color of a white towel. She did this even though she had identified the color white many times before. At last the gorilla plucked a bit of red lint from the towel and showed it to her trainer (Patterson and Linden 80-81). At Yerkes Primate Center, chimpanzees Sherman and Austin, who had been taught symbols for foods and tools, were put in separate rooms. To obtain food in different containers, one chimp had to ask the other for a tool, such as a wrench, by projecting symbols onto a screen using a computer. After some experimentation, the chimpanzees succeeded 97 percent of the time (Marx 1333).

These and hundreds of similar scenes demonstrate that gorillas, orangutans, and chimpanzees resemble humans in language abilities far more than researchers once thought. And evidence is mounting, despite opposition from some linguists and psychologists, that the most intelligent of the apes--pygmy chimpanzees--can understand and perhaps even create sentences.

Although apes lack the vocal ability to produce human sounds, they have acquired vocabularies in American Sign Language and

SAMPLE MLA LIST OF WORKS CITED

Works Cited

Davis, Flora. Eloquent Animals: A Study in
    Animal Communication. New York: Coward,
    1978.

Eckholm, Erik. "Kanzi the Chimp: A Life in
    Science." New York Times 25 June 1985,
    local ed.: C1+.

---. "Pygmy Chimp Readily Learns Language
    Skill." New York Times 24 June 1985, local
    ed.: A1+.

Gibbons, Ann. "Déjà Vu All Over Again: Chimp-
    Language Wars." Science 251 (1991):
    1561-62.

Leakey, Richard, and Roger Lewin. Origins
    Reconsidered: In Search of What Makes Us
    Human. New York: Doubleday, 1992.

Lewin, Roger. "Look Who's Talking Now." New
    Scientist 29 Apr. 1991: 49-52.

Marx, Jean L. "Ape-Language Controversy Flares
    Up." Science 207 (1980): 1330-33.

Patterson, Francine, and Eugene Linden. The
    Education of Koko. New York: Holt, 1981.

Robbins, Esther. Personal interview. 17 Oct.
    1996.

Terrace, H. S., et al. "Can an Ape Create a
    Sentence?" Science 206 (1979): 891-902.

30. ACW style: Documenting Internet sources

The following guidelines for documenting sources retrieved through the Internet are based on a style sheet produced by Janice R. Walker of the University of South Florida and endorsed by the Alliance for Computers and Writing (ACW). They expand on the MLA guidelines for the list of works cited (see 29b) to account for the proliferation of sources available over the Internet. Check with your instructor before following these models; he or she may prefer that you adhere strictly to MLA style.

NOTE: At the end of each entry, put in parentheses the date you accessed the material.

1. FILE TRANSFER PROTOCOL (FTP) SITES

Manning, Gerard. "Celas Worldwide Celtic Music
    Radio Listing." ftp.celtic.stanford.edu
    pub/radio.list (26 Apr. 1996).

2. WORLD WIDE WEB (WWW) SITES

Tómasson, Gunnar. "Anne Hath a Way." <u>Five Notes</u>
    <u>on Shakespeare</u>. http://www.globescope.com/
    ws/will4.htm (26 Feb. 1996).

3. TELNET SITES

Office of Financial Aid, Purdue University. "The
    Loan Counselor." telnet oasis.cc.purdue.edu,
    login: ssinfo,press 5 (5 May 1996).

4. GOPHER SITES

Rifkin, Jeremy. "Vanishing Jobs." Published in
    <u>Mother Jones</u> Sept.-Oct. 1995. gopher
    /mojones.mojones.com/00/SO95/Mother_Jones_
    SO95%3a_Vanishing_Jobs (15 May 1996).

5. NEWSGROUP POSTINGS AND E-MAIL

Catano, Diane. "Transforming Ethics." AAASHRAN@
    gwuvm.gwu.edu (6 Jan. 1996).

```
Wu, Sheila. "Giacometti's Sculpture." Personal
     e-mail (4 Feb. 1996).
```

31. APA documentation style

To document a source, the American Psychological Association (APA) recommends in-text citations that refer readers to a list of references.

DIRECTORY TO APA IN-TEXT CITATIONS

1.	A quotation	123
2.	A summary or a paraphrase	124
3.	Two authors	124
4.	Three to five authors	124
5.	Six or more authors	125
6.	Corporate author	125
7.	Unknown author	125
8.	Authors with the same last name	125
9.	Personal communication	125
10.	Two or more works in the same parentheses	125

31a. APA in-text citations

The APA's in-text citations provide at least the author's last name and the date of publication. For direct quotations, a page number is given as well.

NOTE: In the models that follow, notice that APA style requires the use of the past tense or the present perfect tense in signal phrases introducing material that has been cited: *Smith reported, Smith has argued.*

1. A quotation. Ordinarily, introduce the quotation with a signal phrase that includes the author's last name followed by the date of publication in parentheses. Put the page number in parentheses at the end of the quotation.

```
As Davis (1978) reported, "If the existence of a
signing ape was unsettling for linguists, it was
also startling news for animal behaviorists"
(p. 26).
```

When the author's name does not appear in the signal phrase, place the author's last name, the date, and the page number in parentheses at the end: (Davis, 1978, p. 26).

2. *A summary or a paraphrase.* For a summary or a paraphrase, include the author's last name and the date either in a signal phrase or in parentheses at the end.

According to Davis (1978), when they learned of an ape's ability to use sign language, both linguists and animal behaviorists were taken by surprise.

When they learned of an ape's ability to use sign language, both linguists and animal behaviorists were taken by surprise (Davis, 1978).

NOTE: A page number is not required, but you should provide one if it would help your readers find a specific passage in a long work.

3. *Two authors.* Name both authors in the signal phrase or parentheses each time you cite the work. In the parentheses, use "&" between the authors' names: (Patterson & Linden, 1981). In the signal phrase, use "and."

Patterson and Linden (1981) agreed that the gorilla Koko acquired language more slowly than a normal speaking child.

Koko acquired language more slowly than a normal speaking child (Patterson & Linden, 1981).

4. *Three to five authors.* Identify all authors in the signal phrase or parentheses the first time you cite the source: (Caplow, Bahr, Chadwick, Hill, & Williamson, 1982). In subsequent citations, use the first author's name followed by "et al." in either the signal phrase or parentheses: (Caplow et al., 1982).

5. Six or more authors.   Use only the first author's name followed by "et al." in all citations: (Berger et al., 1971).

6. Corporate author.   If the author is a government agency or other corporate organization with a long and cumbersome name, spell out the name the first time you use it in a citation, followed by an abbreviation in brackets. In later citations, simply use the abbreviation.

FIRST CITATION   (National Institute of Mental

                         Health [NIMH], 1995).

LATER CITATIONS   (NIMH, 1995).

7. Unknown author.   If the author is not given, either use the complete title in a signal phrase or use the first two or three words of the title in the parenthetical citation: ("Strange Encounter," 1987). Titles of articles appear in quotation marks; titles of books are underlined or italicized.

   If "Anonymous" is specified as the author, treat it as if it were a real name: (Anonymous, 1996). In the list of references, also use the name Anonymous as the author.

8. Authors with the same last name.   To avoid confusion, use initials with the last names if your list of references contains two or more authors with the same last name: (J. A. Smith, 1992).

9. Personal communication.   Conversations, memos, letters, e-mail, and similar unpublished person-to-person communications should be cited by initials, last name, and precise date: (L. Smith, personal communication, October 12, 1992). Do not include personal communications in the list of references.

10. Two or more works in the same parentheses. When your parenthetical citation names two or more works, put them in the same order that they appear in the list of references, separated by semicolons: (Berger, 1971; Smith, 1995).

31b. APA list of references

In APA style, the alphabetical list of works cited is titled "References." Following are models illustrating the form that APA recommends for entries in the list of references. Observe all details: capitalization, punctuation, underlining, and so on. For explanations of these matters and for a sample "References" page, see pages 132 and 136.

DIRECTORY TO APA LIST OF REFERENCES

BOOKS

1.	Basic format for a book	127
2.	Two or more authors	127
3.	Corporate author	127
4.	Unknown author	127
5.	Editors	127
6.	Translation	127
7.	Edition other than the first	128
8.	Work in an anthology	128
9.	Multivolume work	128
10.	One volume of a multivolume work	128

PERIODICALS

11.	Article in a magazine	128
12.	Article in a daily newspaper	128
13.	Article in a journal paginated by volume	128
14.	Article in a journal paginated by issue	129
15.	Unsigned article in a periodical	129
16.	Review	129
17.	Letter to the editor	129

OTHER SOURCES

18.	Material from a database	129
19.	CD-ROM abstract	129
20.	Online journal	130
21.	Government document	130
22.	Dissertation abstract	130
23.	Proceedings of a conference	130
24.	Computer program	130
25.	Videotape	131

Books

1. BASIC FORMAT FOR A BOOK

Schaller, G. B. (1993). The last panda. Chicago:
    University of Chicago Press.

2. TWO OR MORE AUTHORS

Eggan, P. D., & Kauchall, D. (1992). Educational
    psychology: Classroom connections. New York:
    Merrill.

Caplow, T., Bahr, H. M., Chadwick, B. A., Hill,
    R., & Williamson, M. H. (1982). Middletown
    families: Fifty years of change and con-
    tinuity. Minneapolis: University of Minne-
    sota Press.

3. CORPORATE AUTHOR

National Institute of Mental Health. (1976).
    Behavior modification: Perspective on a
    current issue. Rockville, MD: Author.

4. UNKNOWN AUTHOR

The Times atlas of the world (9th ed.). (1992).
    New York: Times Books.

5. EDITORS

Fox, R. W., & Lears, T. J. J. (Eds.). (1993).
    The power of culture: Critical essays in
    American history. Chicago: University of
    Chicago Press.

6. TRANSLATION

Miller, A. (1990). The untouched key: Tracing
childhood trauma in creativity and
destructiveness (H. & H. Hannum, Trans.). New
York: Doubleday. (Original work published 1988)

7. EDITION OTHER THAN THE FIRST

Cavanaugh, J. C. (1993). Adult development and
    aging (2nd ed.). Pacific Grove, CA:
    Brooks/Cole.

8. WORK IN AN ANTHOLOGY

Basso, K. H. (1970). Silence in western Apache
    culture. In P. Giglioli (Ed.), Language and
    social context (pp. 67-86). Harmondsworth,
    England: Penguin.

9. MULTIVOLUME WORK

Wiener, P. (Ed.). (1973). Dictionary of the
    history of ideas (Vols. 1-4). New York:
    Scribner's.

10. ONE VOLUME OF A MULTIVOLUME WORK

Wiener, P. (Ed.). (1973). Dictionary of the
    history of ideas (Vol. 2). New York:
    Scribner's.

Periodicals

11. ARTICLE IN A MAGAZINE

Jamison, K. R. (1995, February). Manic-depressive
    illness and creativity. Scientific American,
    272, 62-67.

12. ARTICLE IN A DAILY NEWSPAPER

McGrory, B. (1995, May 23). Pathways to college.
    The Boston Globe, pp. 1, 12-13.

13. ARTICLE IN A JOURNAL PAGINATED BY VOLUME

Block, N. (1992). Begging the question: Against
    phenomenal consciousness. Behavioral and
    Brain Sciences, 15, 205-206.

14. ARTICLE IN A JOURNAL PAGINATED BY ISSUE

Searle, J. (1990). Is the brain a digital
computer? Proceedings of the American
Philosophical Association, 64(3), 21-37.

15. UNSIGNED ARTICLE IN A PERIODICAL

EMFs on the brain. (1995, January 21). Science
News, 141, 44.

16. REVIEW

Blaut, J. M. (1993). [Review of the book Global
capitalism: Theories of societal develop-
ment]. Science and Society, 57(1), 106-107.

17. LETTER TO THE EDITOR

Hopi, M., & Young, J. (1990). European policies
serve to prevent homelessness [Letter to
the editor]. Public Welfare, 48(1), 5-6.

Other sources

18. MATERIAL FROM A DATABASE

Seefeldt, R. W., & Lyon, M. A. (1990, March).
Personality characteristics of adult
children of alcoholics: Fact or fiction?
Paper presented at the annual meeting of
the American Association for Counseling and
Development, Cincinnati, OH. (ERIC Document
Reproduction Service No. ED 316 784)

19. CD-ROM ABSTRACT

Cummings, A. (1995). Test review made easy
[CD-ROM]. Learning, 23(5), 68. Abstract
from: ERIC Document Reproduction Service:
ERIC Item: EJ 509 271

20. ONLINE JOURNAL

Memon, A., & Stevenage, S. (1996, March). Inter-
viewing witnesses: What works and what
doesn't? [32 paragraphs]. Psycoloquy
[On-line serial], 7(6). Available FTP:
Hostname: princeton.edu Directory:
pub/harnad/Psycoloquy/1996.volume.7 File:
psycoloquy.96.7.6.witness-memory.1.memon

21. GOVERNMENT DOCUMENT

U.S. Bureau of the Census. (1989). Statistical
abstract of the United States (109th ed.).
Washington, DC: U.S. Government Printing
Office.

22. DISSERTATION ABSTRACT

Pellman, J. L. (1988). Community integration:
Its influence on the stress of widowhood
(Doctoral dissertation, University of
Missouri, 1988). Dissertation Abstracts
International, 49, 2367.

23. PROCEEDINGS OF A CONFERENCE

Waterhouse, L. H. (1982). Maternal speech
patterns and differential development.
In C. E. Johnson & C. L. Thew (Eds.),
Proceedings of the Second Annual
International Study of Child Language
(pp. 442-454). Washington, DC: University
Press of America.

24. COMPUTER PROGRAM

Notebuilder [Computer software]. (1993). Palo
Alto, CA: Pro/Tem.

25. VIDEOTAPE

National Geographic Society (Producer). (1987).

In the shadow of Vesuvius [Videotape].

Washington, DC: National Geographic Society.

31c. APA manuscript format

In most social science classes, such as psychology, sociology, anthropology, and business, you will be asked to use the APA (American Psychological Association) manuscript format. The following guidelines for manuscript format are based on APA recommendations.

Materials and typeface. Use 8½" × 11" white paper of at least 20-pound weight. For a paper typed on a word processor, make sure that the print quality meets your instructor's standards. Avoid a typeface that is unusual or hard to read.

Margins, spacing, and indentation. Use margins of at least one inch on all sides of the page. If you are working on a word processor, do not justify the right margin.

Double-space throughout the paper, and indent the first line of each paragraph five spaces (one-half inch) from the left margin.

For quotations longer than forty words, indent each line five spaces (one-half inch) from the left margin. Double-space between the body of the paper and the quotation, and double-space between lines in the quotation. Quotation marks are not needed when a quotation is indented.

Page numbers and short title. In the upper right-hand corner of each page, about one-half inch from the top, type a short form of the title of the paper (the first two or three words of the title) followed by five spaces and the page number. Number all pages, including the title page and "References" pages.

Title page. Begin a college paper with a title page. The APA manual does not provide guidelines for the placement of certain information necessary for college papers, but most instructors will want you to supply a title page similar to the one on page 134.

Punctuation and typing.   Although the APA guidelines call for one space after all punctuation, most college professors allow (or even prefer) two spaces at the end of a sentence. Use one space after all other punctuation.

To form a dash, type two hyphens with no space between them. Do not put a space on either side of the dash.

Abstract.   If your instructor requires one, include an abstract immediately after the title page. An abstract is a 75-to-100-word paragraph that provides readers with a quick overview of your essay.

Headings.   For most undergraduate papers, use no more than one or two levels of headings. Center major headings and capitalize the first letter of important words. Do not capitalize minor words — articles, short prepositions, and coordinating conjunctions — unless they are the first word. Type subheadings flush left (against the left margin), underlined or italicized; capitalize as for major headings.

Visuals.   The APA classifies visuals as tables and figures (graphs, charts, drawings, and photographs). Keep visuals as simple as possible. Label each clearly — Table 1, Figure 3, and so on — and include a caption that concisely describes its subject. In the text of your paper, discuss the most significant features of each visual. Ask your instructor for guidelines on placement of visuals in the paper.

Preparing the "References" page

On page 136 is a sample list of references in the APA style. This list, titled "References," begins on a new page at the end of the paper.

In the upper right corner of the page, type the short title of your paper followed by five spaces and the page number. Double-space and center the heading "References" in the width of the page. Double-space throughout.

Unless your instructor suggests otherwise, do not indent the first line of an entry but indent any additional lines five spaces (one-half inch). This technique, known as a "hanging indent," is used for final copy: student papers and actual journal articles. (For manuscripts submitted to journals, APA requires paragraph-style indents that are then converted to hanging indents.)

Alphabetizing the list.   Alphabetize your list by the last names of the authors (or editors); when the author or editor is unknown, alphabetize by the first word of the title other than *A*, *An*, and *The*.

If your list includes two or more works by the same author, arrange the entries by date, the earliest first. If your list includes two or more articles by the same author in the same year, arrange them alphabetically by title. Add lowercase letters beginning with "a," "b," and so on, within the parentheses immediately following the year: (1997a, July 7).

Authors and dates.   Invert all authors' names and use initials instead of first names. With two or more authors, use an ampersand (&). Use all authors' names; do not use "et al."

After the names of the authors, place the date in parentheses.

Titles of books and articles.   Underline the titles and subtitles of books; capitalize only the first word of the title and subtitle (as well as all proper nouns).

Do not place titles of articles in quotation marks, and capitalize only the first word of the title and subtitle (and all proper nouns). Capitalize names of periodicals as you would capitalize them ordinarily. (See section 22.)

The abbreviation "p." (or "pp.").   Abbreviations for "page" or "pages" are used before page numbers of newspaper articles and works in anthologies but not before page numbers of articles appearing in magazines and scholarly journals.

NOTE: The sample "References" page shows you how to type your list of references. For information about the exact format of each entry in your list, consult the models on pages 127–31.

SAMPLE APA TITLE PAGE

Apes and Language:

A Review of the Literature

Karen Shaw

Psychology 110, Section 2

Professor Verdi

April 4, 1996

SAMPLE APA PAGE

Apes and Language:

A Review of the Literature

Over the past twenty-five years, researchers have demonstrated that the great apes (chimpanzees, gorillas, and orangutans) resemble
humans in language abilities more than had been
thought possible. Just how far that resem-
blance extends, however, has been a matter of
some controversy. Researchers agree that the
apes have acquired fairly large vocabularies
in American Sign Language and in artificial
languages, but they have drawn quite different
conclusions in addressing the following questions:

-- How spontaneously have apes used
   language?
-- How creatively have apes used language?
-- Can apes create sentences?
-- What are the implications of the ape
   language studies?

This review of the literature on apes and
language focuses on these four questions.

How Spontaneously Have Apes Used Language?

In an influential article, Terrace, Petitto,
Sanders, and Bever (1979) argued that the apes
in language experiments were not using language
spontaneously, that they were merely imitating
their trainers, responding to conscious or
unconscious cues. Terrace and his colleagues at
Columbia University had trained a chimpanzee,
Nim, in American Sign Language, so their skep-

SAMPLE APA LIST OF REFERENCES

References

Bower, B. (1988). Kanzi extends his speech
      reach. Science News, 134, 140.

Davis, F. (1978). Eloquent animals: A study in
      animal communication. New York: Coward,
      McCann & Geoghegan.

Eckholm, E. (1985a, June 25). Kanzi the chimp:
      A life in science. The New York Times,
      pp. C1, C3.

Eckholm, E. (1985b, June 24). Pygmy chimp
      readily learns language skill. The New York
      Times, pp. A1, B7.

Gibbons, A. (1991). Déjà vu all over again:
      Chimp-language wars. Science, 251,
      1561-1562.

Leakey, R., & Lewin, R. (1992). Origins
      reconsidered: In search of what makes us
      human. New York: Doubleday.

Lewin, R. (1991, April 29). Look who's talking
      now. New Scientist, 130, 49-52.

Patterson, F., & Linden, E. (1981). The
      education of Koko. New York: Holt, Rinehart
      & Winston.

Terrace, H. S., Petitto, L. A., Sanders, R. J.,
      & Bever, T. G. (1979). Can an ape create a
      sentence? Science, 206, 891-902.

32. *Chicago* documentation style (footnotes or endnotes)

Professors in some disciplines, such as history, prefer footnotes or endnotes to the in-text citations discussed in sections 29 and 31. Notes provide complete publishing information either at the bottom of the page (footnotes) or at the end of the paper (endnotes). A raised arabic numeral in the text indicates that a quotation, paraphrase, or summary has been borrowed from a source; to find the publishing information for that source, readers consult the footnote or endnote with the corresponding number.

Footnotes or endnotes are usually based on *The Chicago Manual of Style* (14th ed., 1993). In *Chicago* style, individual notes are single-spaced, and the first line is indented five spaces (one-half inch); double-spacing separates entries. Notes are numbered consecutively throughout the paper.

TEXT

Governor John Andrew was not allowed to recruit black soldiers out of state. "Ostensibly," writes Peter Burchard, "no recruiting was done outside Massachusetts, but it was an open secret that Andrew's agents were working far and wide."[1]

NOTE

1. Peter Burchard, One Gallant Rush: Robert Gould Shaw and His Brave Black Regiment (New York: St. Martin's Press, 1965), 85.

When you use *Chicago*-style documentation, you will usually be asked to include a bibliography at the end of your paper. See 32c.

32a. First reference to a source

The first time you cite a source, the note should include publishing information for that work as well as the page number on which the specific quotation, paraphrase, or summary may be found. The following models are consistent with guidelines set forth in *The Chicago Manual of Style*, 14th edition.

DIRECTORY TO *CHICAGO*-STYLE NOTES

BOOKS

1. Basic format for a book	139
2. Two or three authors	139
3. Four or more authors	139
4. Unknown author	139
5. Author's name in title	139
6. Edited work without an author	139
7. Edited work with an author	139
8. Translated work	139
9. Edition other than the first	140
10. Untitled volume in a multivolume work	140
11. Titled volume in a multivolume work	140
12. Work in an anthology	140
13. Letter in a published collection	140
14. Work in a series	140
15. Encyclopedia or dictionary	141
16. Biblical reference	141

ARTICLES IN PERIODICALS

17. Article in a journal paginated by volume	141
18. Article in a journal paginated by issue	141
19. Article in a magazine	141
20. Article in a newspaper	141
21. Unsigned article	141
22. Book review	141

ELECTRONIC SOURCES

23. Information service	142
24. Online database	142
25. Electronic journal or bulletin board	142
26. Computer software	142

OTHER SOURCES

27. Government document	142
28. Unpublished dissertation	142
29. Personal communication	142
30. Interview	143
31. Film or videotape	143
32. Sound recording	143
33. Source quoted in another source	143

Books

1. BASIC FORMAT FOR A BOOK

1. James M. McPherson, <u>Battle Cry of Free-dom: The Civil War Era</u> (New York: Oxford University Press, 1988), 87.

2. TWO OR THREE AUTHORS

2. Rudolph O. de la Garza, Z. Anthony Kruszewski, and Tomás A. Arciniega, <u>Chicanos and Native Americans: The Territorial Minorities</u> (Englewood Cliffs, N.J.: Prentice-Hall, 1973), 8.

3. FOUR OR MORE AUTHORS

3. Martin J. Medhurst et al., <u>Cold War Rhetoric: Strategy, Metaphor, and Ideology</u> (New York: Greenwood, 1990), 88.

4. UNKNOWN AUTHOR

4. <u>The Men's League Handbook on Women's Suffrage</u> (London, 1912), 23.

5. AUTHOR'S NAME IN TITLE

5. <u>Long Walk to Freedom: The Autobiography of Nelson Mandela</u> (Boston: Little, Brown, 1995), 435.

6. EDITED WORK WITHOUT AN AUTHOR

6. Marshall Sklare, ed., <u>Understanding American Jewry</u> (New Brunswick, N.J.: Transaction Books, 1982), 49.

7. EDITED WORK WITH AN AUTHOR

7. William L. Riordan, <u>Plunkitt of Tammany Hall</u>, ed. Terrence J. McDonald (Boston: Bedford Books, 1994), 33.

8. TRANSLATED WORK

8. Shintaro Ishihara, <u>The Japan That Can't Say No</u>, trans. Frank Baldwin (New York: Simon and Schuster, 1989), 65-83.

9. EDITION OTHER THAN THE FIRST

9. C. H. Lawrence, <u>Medieval Monasticism:
Forms of Religious Life in Western Europe in the
Middle Ages</u>, 2d ed. (London: Longman, 1989),
163-64.

10. UNTITLED VOLUME IN A MULTIVOLUME WORK

10. <u>New Cambridge Modern History</u>
(Cambridge: Cambridge University Press, 1957),
1:52-53.

11. TITLED VOLUME IN A MULTIVOLUME WORK

11. William Wood and Ralph Henry Gabriel,
<u>In Defense of Liberty</u>, vol. 7 of <u>The Pageant of
America</u> (New York: United States Publishers,
1928), 135-42.

or

11. William Wood and Ralph Henry Gabriel,
<u>The Pageant of America</u>, vol. 7, <u>In Defense of
Liberty</u> (New York: United States Publishers,
1928), 135-42.

12. WORK IN AN ANTHOLOGY

12. Michelle T. Clinton, "For Strong
Women," in <u>Home Girls: A Black Feminist An-
thology</u>, ed. Barbara Smith (New York: Kitchen
Table, 1983), 325-27.

13. LETTER IN A PUBLISHED COLLECTION

13. James Thurber to Harold Ross, 27 Decem-
ber 1948, <u>Selected Letters of James Thurber</u>, ed.
Helen Thurber and Edward Weeks (Boston: Little,
Brown, 1981), 65-66.

14. WORK IN A SERIES

14. Robert M. Laughlin, <u>Of Cabbages and
Kings: Tales from Zinacantán</u>, Smithsonian
Contributions to Anthropology, vol. 23 (Washington, D.C.: Smithsonian Institution Press, 1977),
14.

15. ENCYCLOPEDIA OR DICTIONARY

15. <u>Encyclopaedia Britannica</u>, 15th ed., s.v. "evolution."

NOTE: The abbreviation "s.v." is for the Latin *sub verbo* ("under the word").

16. BIBLICAL REFERENCE

16. Matt. 20.4-9 Revised Standard Version.

Articles in periodicals

17. ARTICLE IN A JOURNAL PAGINATED BY VOLUME

17. Laura E. Hein, "In Search of Peace and Democracy: Postwar Japanese Economic Debate in Political Context," <u>Journal of Asian Studies</u> 53 (1994): 752.

18. ARTICLE IN A JOURNAL PAGINATED BY ISSUE

18. Robert Darnton, "The Pursuit of Happiness," <u>Wilson Quarterly</u> 19, no. 4 (1995): 42.

19. ARTICLE IN A MAGAZINE

19. Andrew Weil, "The New Politics of Coca," <u>New Yorker</u>, 15 May 1995, 70.

20. ARTICLE IN A NEWSPAPER

20. Lena H. Sun, "Chinese Feel the Strain of a New Society," <u>Washington Post</u>, 13 June 1993, sec. A.

21. UNSIGNED ARTICLE

21. "Radiation in Russia," <u>U.S. News and World Report</u>, 9 August 1993, 41.

22. BOOK REVIEW

22. Dauril Alden, review of <u>Vanguard of Empire: Ships of Exploration in the Age of Columbus</u>, by Roger C. Smith, <u>Journal of World History</u> 6 (1995): 137.

Electronic sources

23. INFORMATION SERVICE

23. Paul D. Hightower, "Censorship," <u>Con-
temporary Education</u> (Terre Haute: Indiana State
University, School of Education, winter 1995),
66, Dialog, ERIC, ED 509251.

24. ONLINE DATABASE

24. "The Formation of Latin Christendom:
The Roman Church," in EuroDocs: Primary Historical Documents from Western Europe [data-
base online] (Provo, Utah: Brigham Young University, 1996- [cited 10 April 1996]); available
from http://www.fordham.edu/halsall/sbook.html
#romchurch.

25. ELECTRONIC JOURNAL OR BULLETIN BOARD

25. Laura L. Howes, review of <u>Women and
Literature in Britain, 1150-1500</u>, ed. Carol M.
Meale, in <u>Bryn Mawr Medieval Review</u> [electronic
journal] (Cambridge: Cambridge University Press,
1993- [cited 5 March 1996]), file no. 96.1.4;
available from listserv@cc.brynmawr.edu; Internet.

26. COMPUTER SOFTWARE

26. Lotus 1-2-3 Rel. 4, Lotus Development
Corporation, Cambridge, Mass.

Other sources

27. GOVERNMENT DOCUMENT

27. U.S. Department of State, <u>Foreign
Relations of the United States: Diplomatic
Papers, 1943</u> (Washington, D.C.: GPO, 1965), 562.

28. UNPUBLISHED DISSERTATION

28. Cheryl D. Hoover, "East Germany's
Revolution" (Ph.D. diss., Ohio State University,
1994), 450-51.

29. PERSONAL COMMUNICATION

29. Sara Lehman, letter to author, 13
August 1996.

30. Hector LaForge, telephone interview by author, 4 April 1996.

31. Martha Carlin, e-mail to author, 18 June 1996.

30. INTERVIEW

32. Jesse Jackson, interview by Marshall Frady, <u>Frontline</u>, Public Broadcasting System, 30 April 1996.

31. FILM OR VIDEOTAPE

33. <u>North by Northwest</u>, prod. and dir. Alfred Hitchcock, 2 hr. 17 min., MGM/UA, 1959, videocassette.

32. SOUND RECORDING

34. Gustav Holst, <u>The Planets</u>, Royal Philharmonic Orchestra, André Previn, Telarc compact disk 80133.

33. SOURCE QUOTED IN ANOTHER SOURCE

35. George Harmon Knoles, <u>The Jazz Age Revisited: British Criticism of American Civilization during the 1920s</u> (Stanford: Stanford University Press, 1955), 31, quoted in C. Vann Woodward, <u>The Old World's New World</u> (Oxford: Oxford University Press, 1991), 46.

32b. Subsequent references to a source

When citing a work that has already been cited, you may use a shortened note. In most cases, simply give the author's last name, followed by a comma and the page or pages cited.

2. Patterson, 31.

If you cite more than one work by the same author, include a short form of the title in your subsequent citation. A short form of the title of a book is underlined or italicized; a short form of the title of an article is put in quotation marks.

2. Patterson, <u>Slavery</u>, 31.

3. Patterson, "Affirmative Action," 10.

The Chicago Manual of Style allows but does not require the use of "ibid." to refer to the work cited in the previous note. If you are citing the same page of the work, use "ibid." alone. If you are citing a different page, use "ibid." followed by a comma and the page number.

    4. Ibid.

    5. Ibid., 64.

The Latin abbreviations "op. cit." and "loc. cit." are no longer used.

32c. *Chicago*-style bibliography

A bibliography, which appears at the end of your paper, lists every work you have cited in your notes; in addition, it may include works that you consulted but did not cite. For advice on constructing the list, see page 150. A sample bibliography appears on page 155.

The following models are based on guidelines set forth in *The Chicago Manual of Style*, 14th edition.

DIRECTORY TO *CHICAGO*-STYLE BIBLIOGRAPHY

BOOKS

  1. Basic format for a book   145
  2. Two or three authors   145
  3. Four or more authors   145
  4. Unknown author   145
  5. Author's name in title   146
  6. Edited work without an author   146
  7. Edited work with an author   146
  8. Translated work   146
  9. Edition other than the first   146
10. Untitled volume in a multivolume work   146
11. Titled volume in a multivolume work   146
12. Work in an anthology   147
13. Letter in a published collection   147
14. Work in a series   147
15. Encyclopedia or dictionary   147
16. Biblical reference   147

ARTICLES IN PERIODICALS

17. Article in a journal paginated by volume   147
18. Article in a journal paginated by issue   147
19. Article in a magazine   147
20. Article in a newspaper   148
21. Unsigned article   148
22. Book review   148

ELECTRONIC SOURCES

23. Information service   148
24. Online database   148
25. Electronic journal or bulletin board   148
26. Computer software   149

OTHER SOURCES

27. Government document   149
28. Unpublished dissertation   149
29. Personal communication   149
30. Interview   149
31. Film or videotape   149
32. Sound recording   149
33. Source quoted in another source   149

1. BASIC FORMAT FOR A BOOK

McPherson, James M. Battle Cry of Freedom: The
     Civil War Era. New York: Oxford University
     Press, 1988.

2. TWO OR THREE AUTHORS

Garza, Rudolph O. de la, Anthony Kruszewski, and
     Tomás A. Arciniega. Chicanos and Native
     Americans: The Territorial Minorities.
     Englewood Cliffs, N.J.: Prentice-Hall, 1973.

3. FOUR OR MORE AUTHORS

Medhurst, Martin J., et al. Cold War Rhetoric:
     Strategy, Metaphor, and Ideology. New York:
     Greenwood, 1990.

4. UNKNOWN AUTHOR

The Men's League Handbook on Women's Suffrage.
     London, 1912.

5. AUTHOR'S NAME IN TITLE

Mandela, Nelson. <u>Long Walk to Freedom: The Autobiography of Nelson Mandela</u>. Boston:
Little, Brown, 1995.

6. EDITED WORK WITHOUT AN AUTHOR

Sklare, Marshall, ed. <u>Understanding American
Jewry</u>. New Brunswick, N.J.: Transaction
Books, 1982.

7. EDITED WORK WITH AN AUTHOR

Riordan, William L. <u>Plunkitt of Tammany Hall</u>.
Edited by Terrence J. McDonald. Boston:
Bedford Books, 1994.

8. TRANSLATED WORK

Ishihara, Shintaro. <u>The Japan That Can't Say No</u>.
Translated by Frank Baldwin. New York:
Simon and Schuster, 1989.

9. EDITION OTHER THAN THE FIRST

Lawrence, C. H. <u>Medieval Monasticism: Forms of
Religious Life in Western Europe in the
Middle Ages</u>. 2d ed. London: Longman, 1989.

10. UNTITLED VOLUME IN A MULTIVOLUME WORK

<u>New Cambridge Modern History</u>. Vol. 1. Cambridge:
Cambridge University Press, 1957.

11. TITLED VOLUME IN A MULTIVOLUME WORK

Wood, William, and Ralph Henry Gabriel. <u>In
Defense of Liberty</u>. Vol. 7 of <u>The Pageant
of America</u>. New York: United States
Publishers, 1928.

or

Wood, William, and Ralph Henry Gabriel. <u>The
Pageant of America</u>. Vol. 7, <u>In Defense of
Liberty</u>. New York: United States Publishers,
1928.

12. WORK IN AN ANTHOLOGY

Clinton, Michelle T. "For Strong Women." In Home
Girls: A Black Feminist Anthology, edited
by Barbara Smith. New York: Kitchen Table,
1983.

13. LETTER IN A PUBLISHED COLLECTION

Thurber, James. Letter to Harold Ross, 27 Decem-
ber 1948. In Selected Letters of James
Thurber, edited by Helen Thurber and Edward
Weeks, 65-66. Boston: Little, Brown, 1981.

14. WORK IN A SERIES

Laughlin, Robert M. Of Cabbages and Kings: Tales
from Zinacantán. Smithsonian Contributions
to Anthropology, vol. 23. Washington, D.C.:
Smithsonian Institution Press, 1977.

15. ENCYCLOPEDIA OR DICTIONARY
Encyclopedias and dictionaries are usually not included
in the bibliography.

16. BIBLICAL REFERENCE
The Bible is usually not included in the bibliography.

Articles in periodicals

17. ARTICLE IN A JOURNAL PAGINATED BY VOLUME

Hein, Laura E. "In Search of Peace and Democracy: Postwar Japanese Economic Debate
in Political Context." Journal of Asian
Studies 53 (1994): 752-78.

18. ARTICLE IN A JOURNAL PAGINATED BY ISSUE

Darnton, Robert. "The Pursuit of Happiness."
Wilson Quarterly 19, no. 4 (1995): 42-52.

19. ARTICLE IN A MAGAZINE

Weil, Andrew. "The New Politics of Coca." New
Yorker, 15 May 1995, 70.

20. ARTICLE IN A NEWSPAPER

Sun, Lena H. "Chinese Feel the Strain of a New
    Society." <u>Washington Post</u>, 13 June 1993,
    sec. A.

21. UNSIGNED ARTICLE

"Radiation in Russia." <u>U.S. News and World
    Report</u>, 9 August 1993, 40-42.

22. BOOK REVIEW

Alden, Dauril. Review of <u>Vanguard of Empire:
    Ships of Exploration in the Age of
    Columbus</u>, by Roger C. Smith. <u>Journal of
    World History</u> 6 (1995): 137-39.

Electronic sources

23. INFORMATION SERVICE

Hightower, Paul D. "Censorship." <u>Contemporary
    Education</u>. Terre Haute: Indiana State
    University, School of Education, winter
    1995. 66, Dialog, ERIC, ED 509251.

24. ONLINE DATABASE

"The Formation of Latin Christendom: The Roman
    Church." In EuroDocs: Primary Historical
    Documents from Western Europe [database
    online]. Provo, Utah: Brigham Young
    University, 1996- [cited 10 April 1996].
    Available from http://www.fordham.edu/
    halsall/sbook.html#romchurch.

25. ELECTRONIC JOURNAL OR BULLETIN BOARD

Howes, Laura L. Review of <u>Women and Litera-
    ture in Britain, 1150-1500</u>, edited by
    Carol M. Meale. In <u>Bryn Mawr Medieval
    Review</u> [electronic journal]. Cambridge:
    Cambridge University Press, 1993- [cited
    5 March 1996]. File no. 96.1.4. Avail-
    able from listserv@cc.brynmawr.edu;
    Internet.

26. COMPUTER SOFTWARE

Lotus 1-2-3 Rel. 4. Lotus Development Corporation, Cambridge, Mass.

Other sources

27. GOVERNMENT DOCUMENT

U.S. Department of State. Foreign Relations of the United States: Diplomatic Papers, 1943. Washington, D.C.: GPO, 1965.

28. UNPUBLISHED DISSERTATION

Hoover, Cheryl D. "East Germany's Revolution." Ph.D. diss., Ohio State University, 1994.

29. PERSONAL COMMUNICATION
Personal communications are not included in the bibliography.

30. INTERVIEW

Jackson, Jesse. Interview by Marshall Frady. Frontline. Public Broadcasting System, 30 April 1996.

31. FILM OR VIDEOTAPE

North by Northwest. Produced and directed by Alfred Hitchcock. 2 hr. 17 min. MGM/UA, 1959. Videocassette.

32. SOUND RECORDING

Holst, Gustav. The Planets. Royal Philharmonic Orchestra. André Previn. Telarc compact disk 80133.

33. SOURCE QUOTED IN ANOTHER SOURCE

Knoles, George Harmon. The Jazz Age Revisited: British Criticism of American Civilization during the 1920s, 31. Stanford: Stanford University Press, 1955. Quoted in C. Vann Woodward, The Old World's New World (Oxford: Oxford University Press, 1991), 46.

32d. *Chicago*-style manuscript format

The following guidelines on manuscript formatting are based on *The Chicago Manual of Style,* 14th edition.

Title and identification. On the title page, include the full title of your paper and your name. Your instructor may also want you to include the course title, the instructor's name, and the date. Do not type a number on the title page but count it in the manuscript; that is, the first page of text will usually be numbered page 2. In the unusual case that your paper includes extensive preliminary material such as a table of contents, list of illustrations, or preface, you may be required to number that material separately. See page 152 for a sample title page.

Margins and spacing. Leave margins of at least one inch at the top, bottom, and sides of the page. Double-space the entire manuscript, including block quotations, but single-space individual entries in notes and the bibliography.

Pagination. Using arabic numerals, number all pages except the title page in the upper right corner. Depending on your instructor's preference, you may also use a short title or your last name before page numbers to help identify pages in case they come loose from your manuscript.

Preparing the "Notes" page

On page 154 are sample endnotes for a paper in *Chicago* style. (You may choose to or be required to use footnotes instead.) Endnote pages should be numbered consecutively with the rest of the manuscript, and the title "Notes" should be centered on the first page. Indent only the first line of each entry five spaces (one-half inch) and begin the note with the arabic numeral corresponding to the number in the text. Follow the number with a period and one space. Do not indent any other lines of the entry. Single-space individual notes but double-space between notes.

Authors and dates. Authors' names are not inverted in notes. With two or more authors, use "and," not an ampersand (&). In notes for works with four or more authors, use the first author's name followed by "et al."

Page numbers. Page numbers are not preceded by the abbreviation "p." or "pp."

Preparing the "Bibliography" page

Typically, the notes in *Chicago*-style papers are followed by a bibliography, an alphabetically arranged list of all of the works cited or consulted. Page 155 shows a sample bibliography in *Chicago* style.

Type the title "Bibliography," centered, about one inch from the top of the page. Number "Bibliography" pages consecutively with the rest of the paper. Begin each entry at the left margin, and indent any additional lines five spaces (one-half inch). Single-space individual entries but double-space between entries.

Alphabetizing the list. Alphabetize the bibliography by the last names of the authors (or editors); when a work has no author or editor, alphabetize by the first word of the title other than *A*, *An*, and *The*.

If your list includes two or more works by the same author, use three dashes (or three hyphens) instead of the author's name in all entries after the first. You may arrange the entries alphabetically by title or chronologically; be consistent throughout the bibliography.

Authors and dates. Invert the name of the first author or editor. With two or more authors, use "and," not an ampersand (&). For works with four or more authors, use the first author's name, inverted, followed by "et al."

NOTE: The sample "Notes" and "Bibliography" pages show you how to type bibliographic information for *Chicago*-style papers. For more information about the exact format of notes, see 32a; for "Bibliography" entries, see 32c.

The Forgotten Pioneers:
African Americans on the Western Frontier

Robert Diaz

History 120
Professor Marshall
3 October 1996

Most Americans know something of Billy the Kid, Sitting Bull, and General Custer; their lives have been featured as subjects of high school lectures as well as books, films, and TV dramas. But how many people have heard of Clara Brown, an African American who helped bring groups of her people west by wagon train, or of Bill Pickett, a black cowboy who was one of the most famous rodeo riders in the United States?[1] How many know of the "Buffalo soldiers," black cavalrymen who rode and fought on the western plains?[2] Until recently, the role of African Americans in the settlement of the West has been largely ignored in schools and in the media. A growing body of historical research, however, has pointed out the significance of African Americans to the westward development of the United States.

From the American Revolution to the turn of the twentieth century, thousands of African Americans headed west looking for opportunity and a new start in a new land, hoping to escape slavery and racist conditions in the East. They often discovered, however, that discriminatory attitudes had preceded them. As William Lorenz Katz writes, the white pioneers who headed west "carried the virus of racism with them, as much a part of their psyche as their heralded courage and their fears."[3] In the nineteenth century, white settlers from Oklahoma to California were quick to pass segregationist laws in the newly settled territories, and even antislavery laws

SAMPLE *CHICAGO* ENDNOTES

Notes

1. Ruth Pelz, Black Heroes of the Wild West (Seattle: Open Hand Publishing, 1990), 15-36.

2. William H. Leckie, The Buffalo Soldiers (Norman: University of Oklahoma Press, 1967), 5.

3. William Lorenz Katz, The Black West: A Pictorial History, 3d ed. (Seattle: Open Hand Publishing, 1987), 307.

4. Ibid.

5. William Lorenz Katz, The Westward Movement and Abolitionism (Austin: Steck-Vaughn Publishers, Raintree, 1992), 32.

6. Scott Minerbrook, "The Forgotten Pioneers," U.S. News and World Report, 8 August 1994, 53.

7. Katz, Black West, 49.

8. Ginia Bellafante, "Wild West 101," Time, 22 February 1993, 75.

9. John Mack Faragher, "The Frontier Trail: Rethinking Turner and Reimagining the American West," American Historical Review 98 (1993): 106-7.

10. Ibid., 110.

11. Bellafante, 75.

12. Kenneth W. Porter, The Negro on the American Frontier (New York: Arno Press, 1971), 42-45.

13. Ibid., 60.

14. Faragher, 107.

SAMPLE *CHICAGO* BIBLIOGRAPHY

Bibliography

Bellafante, Ginia. "Wild West 101." Time, 22
     February 1993, 75.

Crouch, Barry A. The Freedmen's Bureau and Black
     Texans. Austin: University of Texas Press,
     1992.

Dolan, Edward F. Famous Builders of California.
     New York: Dodd, Mead, 1924.

Faragher, John Mack. "The Frontier Trail:
     Rethinking Turner and Reimagining the
     American West." American Historical Review
     98 (1993): 106-17.

Katz, William Lorenz. The Black West: A Pictor-
     ial History. 3d ed. Seattle: Open Hand
     Publishing, 1987.

---. The Westward Movement and Abolitionism.
     Austin: Steck-Vaughn Publishers, Raintree,
     1992.

Leckie, William H. The Buffalo Soldiers. Norman:
     University of Oklahoma Press, 1967.

Minerbrook, Scott. "The Forgotten Pioneers."
     U.S. News and World Report, 8 August 1994,
     53-55.

Pelz, Ruth. Black Heroes of the Wild West.
     Seattle: Open Hand Publishing, 1990.

Porter, Kenneth W. The Negro on the American
     Frontier. New York: Arno Press, 1971.

Wheeler, B. Gordon. Black California: The
     History of African Americans in the Golden
     State. New York: Hippocrene Books, 1993.

33. A list of style manuals

A Pocket Style Manual describes three commonly used systems of documentation: MLA style, used in English and the humanities (see section 29); APA style, used in psychology and the social sciences (see section 31); and *Chicago*-style footnotes and endnotes (see section 32). Following is a list of style manuals used in a variety of disciplines.

BIOLOGY

Council of Biology Editors. *Scientific Style and Format: The CBE Manual for Authors, Editors, and Publishers.* 6th ed. New York: Cambridge UP, 1994.

CHEMISTRY

Dodd, Janet S., ed. *The ACS Style Guide: A Manual for Authors and Editors.* Washington: Amer. Chemical Soc., 1986.

ENGLISH AND THE HUMANITIES

Gibaldi, Joseph. *MLA Handbook for Writers of Research Papers.* 4th ed. New York: MLA, 1995.

GEOLOGY

Bates, Robert L., Rex Buchanan, and Marla Adkins-Heljeson, eds. *Geowriting: A Guide to Writing, Editing, and Printing in Earth Science.* 5th ed. Alexandria: Amer. Geological Inst., 1992.

HISTORY

The Chicago Manual of Style. 14th ed. Chicago: U of Chicago P, 1993.

LAW

Columbia Law Review. *A Uniform System of Citation.* 16th ed. Cambridge: Harvard Law Review, 1996.

LINGUISTICS

Linguistic Society of America. "LSA Style Sheet." Published annually in the December issue of the *LSA Bulletin.*

MATHEMATICS

American Mathematical Society. *The AMS Author Handbook: General Instructions for Preparing Manuscripts.* Providence: AMS, 1994.

MEDICINE

Iverson, Cheryl, et al. *American Medical Association Manual of Style*. 8th ed. Baltimore: Williams and Wilkins, 1989.

MUSIC

Holoman, D. Kern, ed. *Writing about Music: A Style Sheet from the Editors of* 19th-Century Music. Berkeley: U of California P, 1988.

PHYSICS

American Institute of Physics. *Style Manual: Instructions to Authors and Volume Editors for the Preparation of AIP Book Manuscripts*. 5th ed. New York: AIP, 1995.

POLITICAL SCIENCE

American Political Science Association. *Style Manual for Political Science*. Rev. ed. Washington: Amer. Political Science Assn., 1993.

PSYCHOLOGY AND THE SOCIAL SCIENCES

American Psychological Association. *Publication Manual of the American Psychological Association*. 4th ed. Washington: APA, 1994.

SCIENCE – GENERAL

American National Standard for the Preparation of Scientific Papers for Written or Oral Presentation. New York: Amer. National Standards Inst., 1979.

SOCIAL WORK

National Association of Social Workers. *Writing for NASW*. 2nd ed. Silver Spring: National Assn. of Social Workers, 1994.

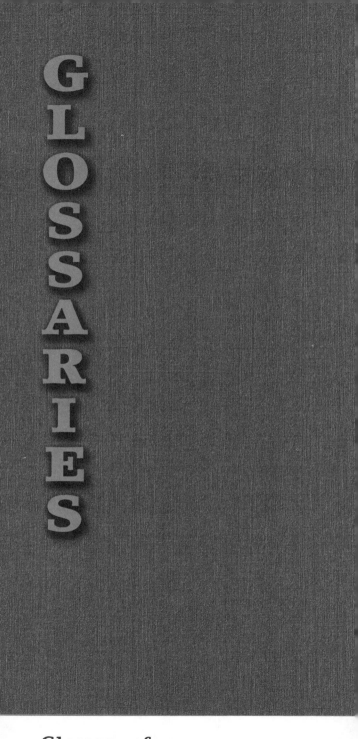

GLOSSARIES

Glossary of usage
Glossary of grammatical terms

34. Glossary of usage

This glossary includes words commonly confused, words commonly misused, and words that are nonstandard. It also lists colloquialisms that may be appropriate in informal speech but are often considered inappropriate in formal writing.

a, an Use *an* before a vowel sound, *a* before a consonant sound: *an apple, a peach.* In words beginning with *h,* if the *h* is silent, the word begins with a vowel sound: *an hour, an honorable deed.* If the *h* is pronounced, the word begins with a consonant sound: *a hospital, a hymn, a hotel.*

accept, except *Accept* is a verb meaning "to receive." *Except* is usually a preposition meaning "excluding": *I will accept all the packages except that one. Except* is also a verb meaning "to exclude": *Please except that item from the list.*

advice, advise *Advice* is a noun, *advise* a verb: *We advise you to follow John's advice.*

affect, effect *Affect* is usually a verb meaning "to influence." *Effect* is usually a noun meaning "result": *The drug did not affect the disease, and it had several adverse side effects. Effect* can also be a verb meaning "to bring about": *Only the president can effect such a dramatic change.*

all ready, already *All ready* means "completely prepared." *Already* means "previously": *Susan was all ready for the concert, but her friends had already left.*

all right *All right* is always written as two words. *Alright* is nonstandard.

all together, altogether *All together* means "everyone gathered." *Altogether* means "entirely": *We were not altogether certain that we could bring the family all together for the reunion.*

allusion, illusion An *allusion* is an indirect reference; an *illusion* is a misconception or false impression: *Did you catch my allusion to Shakespeare? Mirrors give the room an illusion of depth.*

a lot *A lot* is two words. Do not write *alot.*

among, between Ordinarily, use *among* with three or more entities, *between* with two: *The prize was divided among several contestants. You have a choice between carrots and beans.*

amount, number Use *amount* with quantities that cannot be counted; use *number* with those that can: *This recipe* *calls for a large amount of sugar. We have a large number of toads in our garden.*

an See *a, an.*

and/or Avoid *and/or* except in technical or legal documents.

anxious *Anxious* means "worried" or "apprehensive." In formal writing, avoid using *anxious* to mean "eager": *We are eager* [not *anxious*] *to see your new house.*

anyone, any one *Anyone,* an indefinite pronoun, means "any person at all." *Any one* refers to a particular person or thing in a group: *Anyone from Chicago may choose any one of the games on display.*

anyways, anywheres *Anyways* and *anywheres* are nonstandard for *anyway* and *anywhere.*

as *As* is sometimes used to mean "because." But do not use it if there is any chance of ambiguity: *We canceled the picnic because* [not *as*] *it began raining.* An *as* here could mean "because" or "when."

as, like See *like, as.*

awful The adjective *awful* means "awe-inspiring." Colloquially it is used to mean "terrible" or "bad." The adverb *awfully* is sometimes used in conversation as an intensifier meaning "very." In formal writing, avoid these colloquial uses: *I was very* [not *awfully*] *upset last night.*

awhile, a while *Awhile* is an adverb; it can modify a verb, but it cannot be the object of a preposition such as *for.* The two-word form *a while* is a noun preceded by an article and therefore can be the object of a preposition. *Stay awhile. Stay for a while.*

bad, badly *Bad* is an adjective, *badly* an adverb: *They felt bad about being early and ruining the surprise. Her arm hurt badly after she slid into second.* (See section 13.)

being as, being that *Being as* and *being that* are nonstandard expressions. Write *because* or *since* instead.

beside, besides *Beside* is a preposition meaning "at the side of" or "next to": *Annie Oakley slept with her gun beside her bed. Besides* is a preposition meaning "except" or "in addition to": *No one besides Terrie can have that ice cream. Besides* is also an adverb meaning "in addition": *I'm not hungry; besides, I don't like ice cream.*

between See *among, between.*

bring, take Use *bring* when an object is being transported toward you, *take* when it is being moved away:

Please bring me a glass of water. Please take these maga-zines to Mr. Scott.

burst, bursted; bust, busted *Burst* is an irregular verb meaning "to come open or fly apart suddenly or violently." The past-tense form *bursted* is nonstandard. *Bust* and *busted* are slang for *burst* and, along with *bursted*, should not be used in formal writing.

can, may *Can* is traditionally reserved for ability, *may* for permission: *Can you ski down the advanced slope without falling? May I help you?*

capital, capitol *Capital* refers to a city, *capitol* to a build-ing where lawmakers meet: *The residents of the state capital protested the development plans. The capitol has un-dergone extensive renovations. Capital* also refers to wealth or resources.

cite, site *Cite* means "to quote as an authority or ex-ample." *Site* is usually a noun meaning "a particular place": *He cited the zoning law in his argument against the pro-posed site of the gas station.*

coarse, course *Coarse* means "crude" or "rough in tex-ture": *The coarse weave of the wall hanging gave it a three-dimensional quality. Course* usually refers to a path, a play-ing field, or a unit of study; the expression *of course* means "certainly": *I plan to take a course in car repair this sum-mer. Of course, you are welcome to join me.*

complement, compliment *Complement* is a verb mean-ing "to go with or complete" or a noun meaning "something that completes." *Compliment* as a verb means "to flatter"; as a noun it means "flattering remark": *Her skill at rushing the net complements his skill at volleying. Sheiying's music arrangements receive many compliments.*

conscience, conscious *Conscience* is a noun meaning "moral principles"; *conscious* is an adjective meaning "aware or alert": *Let your conscience be your guide. Were you conscious of his love for you?*

continual, continuous *Continual* means "repeated regu-larly and frequently": *She grew weary of the continual tele-phone calls. Continuous* means "extended or prolonged without interruption": *The broken siren made a continuous wail.*

could care less *Could care less* is a nonstandard expres-sion. Write *couldn't care less* instead.

could of *Could of* is nonstandard for *could have*.

criteria *Criteria* is the plural of *criterion*, which means "a standard, rule, or test on which a judgment or decision can be based": *The only criterion for the job is a willingness to work overtime.*

data *Data* is the plural of *datum,* which means "a fact or proposition." Many writers now treat *data* as singular or plural depending on the meaning of the sentence. Some experts insist, however, that *data* can only be plural: *The new data suggest* [not *suggests*] *that our theory is correct.* The singular form *datum* is rarely used.

different from, different than Ordinarily, write *different from: Your sense of style is different from Jim's.* However, *different than* is acceptable to avoid an awkward construction: *Please let me know if your plans are different than* [to avoid *from what*] *they were six weeks ago.*

don't *Don't* is the contraction for *do not: I don't want any. Don't* should not be used as the contraction for *does not,* which is *doesn't: He doesn't* [not *don't*] *want any.*

double negative Standard English allows two negatives only if a positive meaning is intended: *The runners were not unhappy with their performance.* Double negatives used to emphasize negation are nonstandard: *Jack doesn't have to answer to anybody* [not *nobody*].

due to *Due to* is an adjective phrase and should not be used as a preposition meaning "because of": *The trip was canceled because of* [not *due to*] *lack of interest. Due to* is acceptable as a subject complement and usually follows a form of the verb *be: His success was due to hard work.*

effect See *affect, effect.*

e.g. Use *for example* or *for instance* in formal writing.

enthused As an adjective, *enthusiastic* is preferred: *The children were enthusiastic* [not *enthused*] *about going to the circus.*

etc. Avoid ending a list with *etc.* It is more emphatic to end with an example, and in most contexts readers will understand that the list is not exhaustive. When you don't wish to end with an example, *and so on* is more graceful than *etc.*

everyone, every one *Everyone* is an indefinite pronoun: *Everyone wanted to go. Every one,* the pronoun *one* preceded by the adjective *every,* means "each individual or thing in a particular group." *Every one* is usually followed by *of: Every one of the missing books was found.*

except See *accept, except.*

farther, further *Farther* describes distances: *Detroit is farther from Miami than I thought. Further* suggests quan-

tity or degree: *You extended the curfew further than you
should have.*

fewer, less *Fewer* refers to items that can be counted;
less refers to general amounts: *Fewer people are living in
the city. Please put less sugar in my tea.*

further See *farther, further.*

good, well *Good* is an adjective, *well* an adverb: *He
hasn't felt good about his game since he sprained his wrist
last season. She performed well on the uneven parallel bars.*
(See section 13.)

hanged, hung *Hanged* is the past-tense and past-
participle form of the verb *hang,* meaning "to execute": *The
prisoner was hanged at dawn. Hung* is the past-tense and
past-participle form of the verb *hang,* meaning "to fasten
or suspend": *The stockings were hung by the chimney with
care.*

hardly Avoid expressions such as *can't hardly* and *not
hardly,* which are considered double negatives: *I can* [not
can't] *hardly describe my elation at getting the job.*

he At one time *he* was used to mean "he or she." Today
such usage is inappropriate. See page 16 for alternative
constructions.

hisself *Hisself* is nonstandard. Use *himself.*

hopefully *Hopefully* means "in a hopeful manner": *We
looked hopefully to the future.* Do not use *hopefully* in constructions such as the following: *Hopefully, your daughter
will recover soon.* Indicate who is doing the hoping: *I hope
that your daughter will recover soon.*

hung See *hanged, hung.*

i.e. Use *that is* in formal writing.

illusion See *allusion, illusion.*

impact *Impact* is commonly used as a noun. Avoid using
the expression *impact on* as a verb: *The legislation had an
impact on* [not *impacted on*] *our company's policies.*

imply, infer *Imply* means "to suggest or state indirectly";
infer means "to draw a conclusion": *John implied that he
knew all about computers, but the interviewer inferred that
John was inexperienced.*

in regards to *In regards to* confuses two different
phrases: *in regard to* and *as regards.* Use one or the other:
In regard to [or *As regards*] *the contract, ignore the first
clause.*

irregardless *Irregardless* is nonstandard. Use *regardless.*

is when, is where These mixed constructions are often incorrectly used in definitions: *A run-off election is a second election held to break a tie* [not *is when a second election is held to break a tie*].

it is *It is* is nonstandard when used to mean "there is": *There is* [not *It is*] *a fly in my soup.*

its, it's *Its* is a possessive pronoun; *it's* is a contraction for *it is*: *The dog licked its wound whenever its owner walked into the room. It's a perfect day to walk the twenty-mile trail.*

kind of, sort of Avoid using *kind of* or *sort of* to mean "somewhat": *The movie was a little* [not *kind of*] *boring.* Do not put *a* after either phrase: *That kind of* [not *kind of a*] *salesclerk annoys me.*

lead, led *Lead* is a noun referring to a metal. *Led* is the past tense of the verb *to lead*: *He led me to the treasure.*

learn, teach *Learn* means "to gain knowledge"; *teach* means "to impart knowledge": *I must teach* [not *learn*] *my sister to read.*

leave, let Avoid the nonstandard use of *leave* ("to exit") to mean *let* ("to permit"): *Let* [not *Leave*] *me help you with the dishes.*

less See *fewer, less.*

let, leave See *leave, let.*

liable *Liable* means "obligated" or "responsible." Do not use it to mean "likely": *You're likely* [not *liable*] *to trip if you don't tie your shoelaces.*

lie, lay *Lie* is an intransitive verb meaning "to recline or rest on a surface." Its forms are *lie, lay, lain, lying,* and *lies*. *Lay* is a transitive verb meaning "to put or place." Its forms are *lay, laid, laid, laying,* and *lays.* (See p. 25.)

like, as *Like* is a preposition, not a subordinating conjunction. It should be followed only by a noun or a noun phrase. *As* is a subordinating conjunction that introduces a subordinate clause. In casual speech you may say *She looks like she hasn't slept* or *You don't know her like I do.* But in formal writing, use *as*: *She looks as if she hasn't slept. You don't know her as I do.*

loose, lose *Loose* is an adjective meaning "not securely fastened." *Lose* is a verb meaning "to misplace" or "to not win": *Did you lose your only loose pair of work pants?*

may See *can, may.*

maybe, may be *Maybe* is an adverb meaning "possibly"; *may be* is a verb phrase: *Maybe the sun will shine tomorrow. Tomorrow may be a brighter day.*

may of, might of *May of* and *might of* are nonstandard for *may have* and *might have.*

media, medium *Media* is the plural of *medium*: *Of all the media that cover the Olympics, television is the medium that best captures the spectacle of the events.*

most Avoid *most* to mean "almost": *Almost* [not *Most*] *everyone went to the parade.*

must of See *may of.*

myself *Myself* is a reflexive or intensive pronoun. Reflexive: *I cut myself.* Intensive: *I will drive you myself.* Do not use *myself* in place of *I* or *me*: *He gave the plants to Melinda and me* [not *myself*].

nowheres *Nowheres* is nonstandard for *nowhere.*

number See *amount, number.*

of Use the verb *have,* not the preposition *of,* after the verbs *could, should, would, may, might,* and *must*: *They must have* [not *must of*] *left early.*

off of *Off* is sufficient. Omit *of.*

passed, past *Passed* is the past tense of the verb *to pass*: *Emily passed me another slice of cake.* *Past* usually means "belonging to a former time" or "beyond a time or place": *Our past president spoke until past midnight. The hotel is just past the next intersection.*

plus *Plus* should not be used to join independent clauses: *This raincoat is dirty; moreover* [not *plus*], *it has a hole in it.*

precede, proceed *Precede* means "to come before." *Proceed* means "to go forward": *As we proceeded up the mountain, we noticed fresh tracks in the mud, evidence that a group of hikers had preceded us.*

principal, principle *Principal* is a noun meaning "the head of a school or organization" or "a sum of money." It is also an adjective meaning "most important." *Principle* is a noun meaning "a basic truth or law": *The principal expelled her for three principal reasons. We believe in the principle of equal justice for all.*

proceed, precede See *precede, proceed.*

quote, quotation *Quote* is a verb; *quotation* is a noun. Avoid using *quote* as a shortened form of the noun: *Her quotations* [not *quotes*] *from the* Upanishads *intrigued us.*

real, really *Real* is an adjective; *really* is an adverb. *Real* is sometimes used informally as an adverb, but avoid this use in formal writing: *She was really* [not *real*] *angry.* (See section 13.)

reason is because Use *that* instead of *because: The reason I'm late is that* [not *because*] *my car broke down.*

reason why The expression *reason why* is redundant: *The reason* [not *The reason why*] *Jones lost the election is clear.*

respectfully, respectively *Respectfully* means "showing or marked by respect": *He respectfully submitted his opinion to the judge. Respectively* means "each in the order given": *John, Tom, and Larry were a butcher, a baker, and a lawyer, respectively.*

sensual, sensuous *Sensual* means "gratifying the physical senses," especially those associated with sexual pleasure. *Sensuous* means "pleasing to the senses," especially those involved in the experience of art, music, and nature: *The sensuous music and balmy air led the dancers to more sensual movements.*

set, sit *Set* means "to put" or "to place"; *sit* means "to be seated": *She set the dough in a warm corner of the kitchen. The cat sits in the warmest part of the room.*

should of *Should of* is nonstandard for *should have.*

since Do not use *since* to mean "because" if there is any chance of ambiguity: *Because* [not *Since*] *we won the game, we have been celebrating with a pitcher of beer. Since* here could mean "because" or "from the time that."

sit See *set, sit.*

site, cite See *cite, site.*

sure and *Sure and* is nonstandard for *sure to: Be sure to* [not *sure and*] *bring a gift to the host.*

take See *bring, take.*

than, then *Than* is a conjunction used in comparisons; *then* is an adverb denoting time: *That pizza is more than I can eat. Tom laughed, and then we recognized him.*

that See *who, which, that.*

that, which Many writers reserve *that* for restrictive clauses, *which* for nonrestrictive clauses. (See pp. 54–55.)

theirselves *Theirselves* is nonstandard for *themselves.*

them The use of *them* in place of *those* is nonstandard: *Please send those* [not *them*] *letters to the sponsors.*

there, their, they're *There* is an adverb specifying place; it is also an expletive. Adverb: *Sylvia is lying there unconscious.* Expletive: *There are two plums left. Their* is a possessive pronoun: *Fred and Jane finally washed their car.*

They're is a contraction of *they are: Surprisingly, they're late today.*

they The use of *they* to indicate possession is nonstandard. Use *their* instead: *Cindy and Sam decided to sell their* [not *they*] *boat.*

to, too, two *To* is a preposition; *too* is an adverb; *two* is a number: *Too many of your shots slice to the left, but the last two were right on the mark.*

toward, towards *Toward* and *towards* are generally interchangeable, although *toward* is preferred.

try and *Try and* is nonstandard for *try to: I will try to* [not *try and*] *be better about writing to you.*

unique Avoid expressions such as *most unique, more straight, less perfect, very round.* It is illogical to suggest degrees of such absolute concepts as *unique.*

use to, suppose to *Use to* and *suppose to* are nonstandard for *used to* and *supposed to.*

wait for, wait on *Wait for* means "to be in readiness for" or "await." *Wait on* means "to serve": *We're waiting for* [not *waiting on*] *Ruth before we can leave.*

ways *Ways* is colloquial when used in place of *way* to mean "distance": *The city is a long way* [not *ways*] *from here.*

weather, whether The noun *weather* refers to the state of the atmosphere. *Whether* is a conjunction referring to a choice between alternatives: *We wondered whether the weather would clear up in time for our picnic.*

where Do not use *where* in place of *that: I heard that* [not *where*] *the crime rate is increasing.*

which See *that, which* and *who, which, that.*

while Avoid using *while* to mean "although" or "whereas" if there is any chance of ambiguity: *Although* [not *While*] *Gloria lost money in the slot machine, Tom won it at roulette.* Here *While* could mean either "although" or "at the same time that."

who, which, that Use *who,* not *which,* to refer to persons. Generally, use *that* to refer to things or, occasionally, to a group or class of people: *Fans wondered how an old man who* [not *that* or *which*] *walked with a limp could play football. The team that scores the most points in this game will win the tournament.*

who, whom *Who* is used for subjects and subject complements; *whom* is used for objects. (See pp. 35–36.)

who's, whose *Who's* is a contraction of *who is*; *whose* is a possessive pronoun: *Who's ready for more popcorn? Whose coat is this?*

would of *Would of* is nonstandard for *would have.*

you In formal writing, avoid *you* in an indefinite sense meaning "anyone": *Any spectator* [not *You*] *could tell by the way John caught the ball that his throw would be too late.* (See p. 32.)

your, you're *Your* is a possessive pronoun; *you're* is a contraction of *you are: Is that your new motorcycle? You're on the list of finalists.*

35. Glossary of grammatical terms

This glossary gives definitions for parts of speech, such as nouns; parts of sentences, such as subjects; and types of sentences, clauses, and phrases.

If you are looking up the name of an error (sentence fragment, for example), consult the index or the table of contents instead.

absolute phrase A word group that modifies a whole clause or sentence, usually consisting of a noun followed by a participle or participial phrase: *His tone suggesting no hint of humor,* the minister told us to love our enemies because it would drive them nuts.

active vs. passive voice When a verb is in the active voice, the subject of the sentence does the action: The early *bird catches* the early worm. In the passive voice, the subject receives the action: The early *worm is* sometimes *caught* by the early bird. Often the actor does not appear in the passive-voice sentence: The early *worm is* sometimes *caught.* (See also pp. 3–5 and 28.)

adjective A word used to modify (describe) a noun or pronoun: the *lame* dog, *rare old* stamps, *sixteen* candles. Adjectives usually answer one of these questions: Which one? What kind of? How many or how much? (See also pp. 36–38.)

adjective clause A subordinate clause that modifies a noun or pronoun. An adjective clause begins with a relative pronoun (*who, whom, whose, which, that*) or a relative adverb (*when, where*) and usually appears right after the word it modifies: The arrow *that has left the bow* never returns.

adverb A word used to modify a verb, an adjective, or another adverb: rides *smoothly, unusually* attractive, *very* slowly. An adverb usually answers one of these questions: When? Where? How? Why? Under what conditions? To what degree? (See also pp. 36–37.)

adverb clause A subordinate clause that modifies a verb (or occasionally an adjective or adverb). An adverb clause begins with a subordinating conjunction such as *although, because, if, unless,* or *when* and usually appears at the beginning or the end of a sentence: *When the well is dry,* we know the worth of water. Don't talk *unless you can improve the silence.*

agreement See pages 18–22 and 29–31.

antecedent A noun or pronoun to which a pronoun refers: When the *wheel* squeaks, *it* is greased. *Wheel* is the antecedent of the pronoun *it.*

appositive A noun or noun phrase that renames a nearby noun or pronoun: Politicians, *acrobats at heart,* can lean on both sides of an issue at once.

article The word *a, an, the,* used to mark a noun. (See also pp. 44–47.)

case See pages 33–36.

clause A word group containing a subject, a verb, and any objects, complements, or modifiers of the verb. See *independent clause, subordinate clause.*

complement See *subject complement, object complement.*

complex sentence A sentence consisting of one independent clause and one or more subordinate clauses. In the following example, the subordinate clause is italicized: Do not insult the mother alligator *until you have crossed the river.*

compound-complex sentence A sentence consisting of at least two independent clauses and at least one subordinate clause. In the following example, the subordinate clauses are italicized: Tell me *what you eat,* and I will tell you *what you are.*

compound sentence A sentence consisting of two independent clauses. The clauses are usually joined by a comma and a coordinating conjunction (*and, but, or, nor, for, so, yet*) or by a semicolon: One arrow is easily broken, but you can't break a bundle of ten. Love is blind; envy has its eyes wide open.

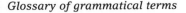

conjunction A joining word. See *coordinating conjunction, correlative conjunction, subordinating conjunction, conjunctive adverb.*

conjunctive adverb An adverb used with a semicolon to connect independent clauses: If an animal does something, we call it instinct; *however,* if we do the same thing, we call it intelligence. The most commonly used conjunctive adverbs are *consequently, furthermore, however, moreover, nevertheless, then, therefore,* and *thus.* See page 60 for a more complete list.

coordinating conjunction One of the following words, used to join elements of equal grammatical rank: *and, but, or, nor, for, so, yet.*

correlative conjunction A pair of conjunctions connecting grammatically equal elements: *either . . . or, neither . . . nor, whether . . . or, not only . . . but also,* and *both . . . and.*

count nouns See pages 44–45.

demonstrative pronoun A pronoun used to identify or point to a noun: *this, that, these, those. This* hanging will surely be a lesson to me.

direct object A word or word group that receives the action of the verb: The little snake studies *the ways of the big serpent.* The complete direct object is *the ways of the big serpent.* The simple direct object is always a noun or pronoun, such as *ways.*

expletive The word *there* or *it* when used at the beginning of a sentence to delay the subject: *There* are many paths to the top of the mountain. *It* is not good to wake a sleeping lion. The delayed subjects are the noun *paths* and the infinitive phrase *to wake a sleeping lion.*

gerund A verb form ending in *-ing,* used as a noun: Continual *dripping* wears away a stone. *Dripping* is used as the subject of the verb *wears away.*

gerund phrase A gerund and its objects, complements, or modifiers. A gerund phrase always functions as a noun, usually as a subject, a subject complement, or a direct object. In the following example, the phrase functions as a subject: *Justifying a fault* doubles it.

helping verb One of the following words, when used with a main verb: *be, am, is, are, was, were, being, been; has, have, had; do, does, did; can, will, shall, should, could, would, may, might, must.* Helping verbs always precede main verbs: *will work, is working, had worked.*

indefinite pronoun A pronoun that refers to a nonspecific person or thing: *Anyone* who serves God for money will serve the Devil for better wages. The most common indefinite pronouns are *all, another, any, anybody, anyone, anything, both, each, either, everybody, everyone, everything, few, many, neither, nobody, none, no one, nothing, one, some, somebody, someone, something.*

independent clause A clause (containing a subject and a verb) that can or does stand alone as a sentence. Every sentence consists of at least one independent clause. In addition, many sentences contain subordinate clauses that function as adjectives, adverbs, or nouns. See also *subordinate clause.*

indirect object A noun or pronoun that names to whom or for whom the action is done: Fate gives *us* our relatives. An indirect object always precedes a direct object, in this case *our relatives.*

infinitive The word *to* followed by a verb: *to think, to dream.*

infinitive phrase An infinitive and its objects, complements, or modifiers. An infinitive phrase can function as a noun, an adjective, or an adverb: *To side with truth* is noble. We do not have the right *to abandon the poor.* Do not use a hatchet *to remove a fly from your friend's forehead.*

intensive or reflexive pronoun A pronoun ending in -*self: myself, yourself, himself, herself, itself, ourselves, yourselves, themselves.* An intensive pronoun emphasizes a noun or another pronoun: I *myself* don't understand my moods. A reflexive pronoun names a receiver of an action identical with the doer of the action: Did you cut *yourself?*

interjection A word expressing surprise or emotion: *Oh! Wow! Hey! Hooray!*

interrogative pronoun A pronoun used to open a question: *who, whom, whose, which, what. What* does history teach us?

intransitive verb See *transitive and intransitive verbs.*

irregular verb See *regular and irregular verbs.* Or see pages 22–25.

linking verb A verb that links a subject to a subject complement, a word or word group that renames or describes the subject: Prejudice *is* the child of ignorance. Good medicine sometimes *tastes* bitter. The most common linking verbs are forms of *be: be, am, is, are, was, were, being, been.*

The following verbs sometimes function as linking verbs: *appear, become, feel, grow, look, make, seem, smell, sound, taste.*

modifier A word, phrase, or clause that describes or qualifies the meaning of a word. Modifiers include adjectives, adverbs, prepositional phrases, participial phrases, some infinitive phrases, and adjective and adverb clauses.

mood See page 28.

noun The name of a person, place, or thing: The *cat* in *gloves* catches no *mice.* Nouns are classified for a variety of purposes. When capitalization is the issue, we speak of *proper* versus *common* nouns (see pp. 74–75). If the problem involves the use of articles, we distinguish between *count* nouns and *noncount* nouns (see pp. 44–45). Most nouns come in *singular* and *plural* forms; *collective nouns* may be either singular or plural (see pp. 20, 21–22). *Possessive* nouns require an apostrophe (see pp. 63–64).

noun clause A subordinate clause that functions as a noun, usually as a subject, a subject complement, or a direct object. In the following sentence, the italicized noun clauses function as subject and subject complement: *What history teaches us* is *that we have never learned anything from it.* Noun clauses usually begin with *how, who, whom, that, what, whether,* or *why.*

noun equivalent A word or word group that functions like a noun: a pronoun, a noun and its modifiers, a gerund phrase, some infinitive phrases, a noun clause.

object See *direct object, indirect object.*

object complement A word or word group that renames or describes a direct object. It always appears after the direct object: Our fears do make us *traitors.* Love makes all hard hearts *gentle.*

object of a preposition See *prepositional phrase.*

participial phrase A present or past participle and its objects, complements, or modifiers. A participial phrase always functions as an adjective describing a noun or pronoun. Usually it appears before or after the word it modifies: *Being weak,* foxes are distinguished by superior tact. Truth *kept in the dark* will never save the world.

participle, past A verb form usually ending in *-d, -ed, -n, -en,* or *-t: asked, spoken, stolen.* Although past participles usually function as main verbs (was *asked,* had *spoken*), they may also be used as adjectives (the *stolen* car).

participle, present A verb form ending in *-ing*. Although present participles usually function as main verbs (is *rising*), they may also be used as adjectives (the *rising* tide).

parts of speech A system for classifying words. Many words can function as more than one part of speech. See *noun, pronoun, verb, adjective, adverb, preposition, conjunction, interjection.*

passive voice See *active vs. passive voice.*

personal pronoun One of the following pronouns, used to refer to a specific person or thing: *I, me, you, she, her, he, him, it, we, us, they, them.* Admonish your friends in private; praise *them* in public.

phrase A word group that lacks a subject, a verb, or both. Most phrases function within sentences as adjectives, as adverbs, or as nouns. See *absolute phrase, appositive, gerund phrase, infinitive phrase, participial phrase, prepositional phrase.*

possessive case See page 33.

possessive pronoun A pronoun used to indicate ownership: *my, mine, your, yours, her, hers, his, its, our, ours, your, yours, their, theirs.* A cock has great influence on his own dunghill.

predicate A verb and any objects, complements, and modifiers that go with it: A clean glove *often hides a dirty hand.*

preposition A word placed before a noun or noun equivalent to form a phrase modifying another word in the sentence. The preposition indicates the relation between the noun (or noun equivalent) and the word the phrase modifies. The most common prepositions are *about, above, across, after, against, along, among, around, at, before, behind, below, beside, besides, between, beyond, by, down, during, except, for, from, in, inside, into, like, near, next, of, off, on, onto, out, outside, over, past, since, than, through, to, toward, under, unlike, until, up, with,* and *without.*

prepositional phrase A phrase beginning with a preposition and ending with a noun or noun equivalent (called the *object of the preposition*). Most prepositional phrases function as adjectives or adverbs. Adjective phrases usually come right after the noun or pronoun they modify: Variety is the spice *of life.* Adverb phrases usually appear at the beginning or the end of the sentence: *To the ant,* a few drops of rain are a flood. Do not judge a tree *by its bark.*

progressive verb forms See pages 26–27.

pronoun   A word used in place of a noun. Usually the pronoun substitutes for a specific noun, known as its antecedent. In the following example, *elephant* is the antecedent of the pronoun *him*: When an *elephant* is in trouble, even a frog will kick *him*. See also *demonstrative pronoun, indefinite pronoun, intensive or reflexive pronoun, interrogative pronoun, personal pronoun, possessive pronoun, relative pronoun*.

regular and irregular verbs   When a verb is regular, both the past tense and past participle are formed by adding *-ed* or *-d* to the base form of the word: *walk, walked, walked*. Irregular verbs are formed in a variety of other ways: *ride, rode, ridden; begin, began, begun; go, went, gone*; and so on. See also pages 22–25.

relative adverb   The word *when* or *where*, when used to introduce an adjective clause.

relative pronoun   One of the following words, when used to introduce an adjective clause: *who, whom, whose, which, that*. A fable is a bridge *that* leads to truth.

sentence   A word group consisting of at least one independent clause. See also *simple sentence, compound sentence, complex sentence, compound-complex sentence*.

simple sentence   A sentence consisting of one independent clause and no subordinate clauses: The frog in the well knows nothing of the ocean.

subject   A word or word group that names who or what the sentence is about. In the following example, the complete subject (the simple subject and all of its modifiers) is italicized: *Historical books that contain no lies* are tedious. The simple subject is *books*. See also *subject after verb, understood subject*.

subject after verb   Although the subject normally precedes the verb, sentences are sometimes inverted. In the following example, the subject *the real tinsel* comes after the verb *lies:* Behind the phony tinsel of Hollywood lies the real tinsel. When a sentence begins with the expletive *there* or *it*, the subject always follows the verb. See *expletive*.

subject complement   A word or word group that follows a linking verb and either renames or describes the subject of the sentence. If the subject complement renames the subject, it is a noun or a noun equivalent: The handwriting on the wall may be *a forgery*. If it describes the subject, it is an adjective: Love is *blind*.

subjunctive mood   See page 28.

subordinate clause A clause (containing a subject and verb) that cannot stand alone as a sentence. Subordinate clauses function within sentences as adjectives, adverbs, or nouns. They begin with subordinating conjuctions such as *although, because, if,* and *until* or with relative pronouns such as *who, which,* and *that.* See *adjective clause, adverb clause, noun clause.*

subordinating conjunction A word that introduces a subordinate clause and indicates its relation to the rest of the sentence. The most common subordinating conjunctions are *after, although, as, as if, because, before, even though, if, since, so that, than, that, though, unless, until, when, where, whether,* and *while.* Note: The relative pronouns *who, whom, whose, which,* and *that* also introduce subordinate clauses.

tenses See pages 25–27.

transitive and intransitive verbs Transitive verbs take direct objects, nouns or noun equivalents that receive the action. In the following example, the transitive verb *loves* takes the direct object *its mother:* A spoiled child never *loves* its mother. Intransitive verbs do not take direct objects: Money *talks.* If any words follow an intransitive verb, they are adverbs or word groups functioning as adverbs: The sun *will set* without your assistance.

understood subject The subject *you* when it is understood but not actually present in the sentence. Understood subjects occur in sentences that issue commands or advice: [*You*] Hitch your wagon to a star.

verb A word that expresses action (*jump, think*) or being (*is, was*). A sentence's verb is composed of a main verb possibly preceded by one or more helping verbs: The best fish *swim* near the bottom. A marriage *is* not *built* in a day. Verbs have five forms: the base form, or dictionary form (*walk, ride*), the past-tense form (*walked, rode*), the past participle (*walked, ridden*), the present participle (*walking, riding*) and the *-s* form (*walks, rides*).

verbal phrase See *gerund phrase, infinitive phrase, participial phrase.*

Index

a, an, 44, 159
Abbreviations, 76–78
  capitalization of, 76
  periods with, 69
  plurals of, 64
Absolute phrases, 168
  commas with, 56
Abstracts, in APA paper, 132
accept, except, 159
Active verbs, 3–5
Active voice, 3–5, 28, 168
ACW style, for Internet
    sources, 122–23
A.D., B.C., 77
Adjective clauses, 168–69
  ESL problems with, 50
  punctuation of, 54–55
Adjectives, 36–38, 168
  hyphenated, 85
  punctuation of, 53–54
Adverb clauses, 169
  punctuation of, 52–53
Adverbs, 36–38, 169
  relative, 174
advice, advise, 159
affect, effect, 159
Agreement
  pronoun with antecedent,
    29–31
  subject with verb, 18–22
all-, hyphen with, 85
Alliance for Computers and
    Writing. *See* ACW style
all ready, already, 159
all right, 159
all together, altogether, 159
allusion, illusion, 159
almost, placement of, 10
a lot, 159
already, all ready, 159
alright, 159
altogether, all together, 159
am versus *is* or *are,* 18–22
A.M., P.M., a.m., p.m., 77
American Psychological As-
    sociation. *See* APA style
among, between, 159
amount, number, 159–60
an, a, 44, 159
and
  as coordinating conjunc-
    tion, 170
  excessive use of, 13
  parallelism and, 5–6

  punctuation with, 52, 58,
    59
  subjects joined by, 19
and/or, 160
Antecedent, 169
  agreement of pronoun
    and, 29–31
  reference of pronoun to,
    31–32
  of *who, which, that,* 21
anxious, 160
any, 20
anybody, anyone, 19–20,
    29–30
anyone, any one, 160
anyways, anywheres, 160
APA style, 123–36. *See also*
    Researched writing
  in-text citations, 123–25
  manuscript format,
    131–33
  references, 126–31
  sample pages, 134–35
  sample references, 136
Apostrophe, 63–65
Appositives, 169
  case of pronouns with, 34
  punctuation with, 55
Appropriate voice, 14–16
are versus *is,* 18–22
Articles, 169
  a versus *an,* 159
  ESL problems with, 44–47
as
  ambiguous use of, 160
  parallelism and, 6
  pronoun after, 34–35
as, like, 164
Auxiliary verbs. *See* Helping
    verbs
awful, 160
awhile, a while, 160

bad, badly, 38, 160
Base form of verb, 22, 47–48
B.C., A.D., 77
be
  and agreement with
    subject, 18
  as helping verb, 47, 170
  as irregular verb, 24
  as linking verb, 37, 171–72
  in subjunctive mood, 28
  in tenses, 26–27

as weak verb, 3–4
being as, being that, 160
beside, besides, 160
between, among, 159
Biased language, 16
Bible
    no italics for, 80
    punctuation between
        chapter and verse, 62
Bibliography
    APA style (References),
        126–31, 136
    Chicago style, 144–49, 155
    MLA style (Works Cited),
        108–16, 121
Borrowed ideas, 92–93
Brackets, 71–72, 96–97
bring, take, 160–61
burst, bursted, bust, busted,
        161
but. See Coordinating con-
        junctions

can, as modal, 47–48
can, may, 161
can't hardly, 163
capital, capitol, 161
Capitalization, 74–76
    of abbreviations, 76
    in APA references, 133
    after colon, 76
    of first word of sentence,
        75
    proper versus common
        nouns, 74–75
    in quotations, 75–76
    of titles with proper
        nouns, 75
    in titles of works, 75
capitol, capital, 161
Case. *See* Pronoun case
Central idea. *See* Thesis
cf., 78
Chicago Manual of Style, The,
        156
Chicago style, 137–55.
        See also Researched
        writing
    bibliography, 144–49
    footnotes or endnotes,
        137–44
    manuscript format, 150–51
    sample bibliography, 155
    sample notes, 154
    sample pages, 152–53

Choppy sentences, 12–13
Citations. *See* Citing sources
cite, site, 161
Citing sources
    APA style, 123–36
    Chicago style, 137–55
    Internet sources (ACW
        style), 122–23
    MLA style, 103–21
    other styles, 156–57
Clause, 169. *See also*
        Independent clauses;
        Subordinate clauses
coarse, course, 161
Collective nouns, 20, 30–31
Colons, 61–63
    capitalization after, 76
    spacing after, 117–18, 132
    with quotations, 61–62,
        66–67
Commas, 52–58. *See also*
        Commas, unnecessary
    with absolute phrases, 56
    in addresses, 57–58
    after conjunctive adverbs,
        56
    with contrasted elements,
        57
    between coordinate
        adjectives, 53–54
    before coordinating con-
        junctions, 52
    in dates, 57
    with interrogative tags, 57
    after introductory
        elements, 52–53
    with mild interjections, 57
    with nonrestrictive
        elements, 54–55
    with nouns of direct
        address, 57
    with parenthetical
        expressions, 56
    with quotation marks, 57,
        66–68
    in series, 53
    with titles following
        names, 58
    with transitional expres-
        sions, 56
    with *yes* and *no,* 57
Commas, unnecessary, 58–59
Comma splices, 41
Common knowledge, 92–93
Common nouns, 74–75

Comparative form of adjectives and adverbs, 38
Comparisons
  omissions in, 7
  parallel elements in, 6
  with pronoun following *than* or *as*, 34–35
complement, compliment, 161
Complements, object, 172
Complements, subject, 174
  adjectives as, 33–34
  case of, 33–34
Complex sentences, 169
compliment, complement, 161
Compound-complex sentences, 169
Compound elements
  case of pronoun in, 33
  comma with, 52
  no comma with, 58
  omissions in, 6–7
  parallelism and, 5–6
Compound numbers, hyphens with, 85
Compound sentences, 169
Compound subjects, 19
Compound words
  hyphens with, 84–85
  plural of, 82
Conciseness, 2–3
Conjunctions, 170
Conjunctive adverbs, 170
  punctuation with, 43, 56, 60
conscience, conscious, 161
Consistency. *See* Shifts
continual, continuous, 161
Contractions, 64
Coordinate adjectives, 53–54
Coordinating conjunctions, 170
  to correct run-on sentence, 42–43
  parallelism and, 5–6
  punctuation with, 52, 58
Correlative conjunctions, 6, 170
could, as modal, 47–48
could care less, 161
could of, 161
Count nouns, 44–45
course, coarse, 161
criteria, 161–62
Cumulative adjectives, 53–54, 58

Dangling modifiers, 11–12
Dashes, 70–71
data, 162
Dates
  commas with, 57
  numbers in, 78
Demonstrative pronouns, 170
Dependent clauses. *See* Subordinate clauses
Diction. *See* Words
different from, different than, 162
Direct objects, 170
  and case of pronoun, 33
Division of words, 85
do, as helping verb, 47–48
do versus *does. See* Subject-verb agreement
Documentation. *See also* Researched writing
  APA style, 123–36
  Chicago style, 137–55
  Internet sources (ACW style), 122–23
  MLA style, 103–21
  style manuals, list of, 156–57
does, as helping verb, 47–48
does versus *do. See* Subject-verb agreement
don't versus *doesn't,* 162. *See also* Subject-verb agreement
Double negative, 162
Double subject, 50
due to, 162

each, 19–20, 29–30
-ed, verb ending, 22, 49
effect, affect, 159
e.g., 78, 162
either, 19–20, 29–30
either . . . or, 6
-elect, hyphen with, 85
Electronic sources, citing, 115–16, 122–23
Ellipsis mark, 72, 96–97
Emphasis
  active verbs for, 3–5
  italics for, 81
  punctuation for, 70
Endnotes. *See* Footnotes or endnotes

English as a Second
    Language (ESL), 44–50
  articles, 44–47
  helping verbs and main
    verbs, 47–49
  omitted subjects,
    expletives, or verbs,
    49–50
  repeated subjects or
    objects, 50
enthused, 162
ESL. *See* English as a
    Second Language (ESL)
et al., 78
  in *APA* style, 125
  in *Chicago* style, 139, 145
  in *MLA* style, 104, 110
etc., 78, 162
even, placement of, 10
everybody, everyone,
    everything, 19–20, 29–30
everyone, every one, 162
Evidence, 90
ex-, hyphen with, 85
except, accept, 159
Exclamation point, 70
  with quotation marks, 67
Expletives *there, it*, 21,
    49–50, 170

Facts, integrating, 101
farther, further, 162–63
fewer, less, 163
First-person point of view,
    7–8
Footnotes or endnotes,
    123–36. *See also*
    Chicago style
for. See Coordinating con-
    junctions; Prepositions
Foreign words, italics for, 80
Format of manuscript. *See*
    Manuscript formats
Fragments, sentence, 39–41
further, farther, 162–63
Fused sentences, 41
Future perfect tense, 26
Future progressive form, 27
Future tense, 26

Generic nouns, 30
Gerund phrases, 170
Gerunds, 170
  modifier of, 35
good, well, 37, 163

hanged, hung, 163
hardly, 163
has and *have*, as helping
    verbs, 47–48
has versus *have. See* Subject-
    verb agreement
he, him, his, sexist use of, 16,
    163
Helping verbs, 170
  ESL problems with,
    47–49
her versus *she*, 33–35
he/she, his/her, 72
he versus *him*, 33–35
hisself, 163
hopefully, 163
however
  comma after, 56
  semicolon with, 56, 60
hung, hanged, 163
Hyphen, 84–85

I
  point of view, 7–8
  versus *me*, 33–35
i.e., 78, 163
if clauses, 28
illusion, allusion, 159
impact, 163
Imperative mood, 28
imply, infer, 163
Incomplete comparison, 7
Incomplete construction, 6–7
Incomplete sentence. *See*
    Sentence fragments
Indefinite pronouns, 171
  agreement of verb with,
    19–20
  as antecedents, 29–30
  apostrophe with, 64
Indenting
  in *APA* references, 132–33
  in *MLA* works cited, 118
  of quotations, 98
Independent clauses, 171
  punctuation with, 52,
    59–62
Indicative mood, 28
Indirect objects, 171
  and case of pronoun, 33
infer, imply, 163
Infinitive phrases, 171
Infinitives, 171
  case with, 35
  split, 12

-*ing* verb form. *See* Present participle
in regards to, 163
Intensive pronouns, 171
Interjections, 171
  commas with, 57
Internet sources, citing, 115–16, 122–23
Interrogative pronouns, 171
  who, whom, 35–36
In-text citations
  APA style, 123–25
  MLA style, 103–07
Intransitive verbs, 171
Inverted order
  and subject-verb agreement, 20–21
  for variety, 13–14
irregardless, 163
Irregular verbs, 22–25, 171
is versus *are,* 18–22
is when, is where, 164
it
  as expletive, 49–50, 170
  reference of, 32
Italics, 79–81
it is
  ESL problem, 49–50
  nonstandard use, 164
its, it's, 64, 164

Jargon, 14–15
just, placement of, 10

kind of, sort of, 164

Latin abbreviations, 78
lay, lie, 23, 164
lead, led, 164
learn, teach, 164
leave, let, 164
less, fewer, 163
liable, 164
lie, lay, 164
like, as, 164
Linking verbs, 37–38, 171–72
List of works cited. *See* Works cited
Literary present tense, 27
loose, lose, 164

Main clauses. *See* Independent clauses
Main point. *See* Thesis
Main verbs. *See* Verbs

man, 16
Manuscript formats
  APA, 131–33
  Chicago, 150–51
  MLA, 117–18
Mass nouns. *See* Noncount nouns
may, as modal, 47–48
may, can, 161
maybe, may be, 164
may of, might of, 165
media, medium, 165
me versus *I,* 33–35
might, as modal, 47–48
might of, may of, 165
Misplaced modifiers, 10–11
Misspelled words, 83–84
Mixed constructions, 9–10
MLA Handbook for Writers of Research Papers, 156
MLA style, 103–21. *See also* Researched writing
  in-text citations, 103–07
  list of works cited, 108–16
  manuscript format, 117–18
  notes (optional), 116–17
  sample pages, 119–20
  sample works cited, 121
Modals, ESL problems with, 47–48
Modern Language Association. *See* MLA style
Modifiers, 172
  dangling, 11–12
  of gerunds, 35
  misplaced, 10–11
  redundant, 2
Mood of verbs, 28
moreover
  comma after, 56
  semicolon with, 56, 60
most, 165
must, as modal, 47–48
must of, 165
myself, 165

N.B., 78
Negatives, double, 162
neither, 19–20, 29–30
neither . . . nor, 6
Noncount nouns, 44–45
none, 19–20, 29–30
Nonrestrictive elements, 54–55

Nonsexist language, 16, 30
no one, 19–20, 29–30
nor. See Coordinating
    conjunctions
Notes
    Chicago style, 137–44
    MLA style, 116–17
not only . . . but also, 5–6
Noun clauses, 172
Noun equivalent, 172
Nouns, 172. *See also* Nouns,
    types of
    articles with, 44–47
    capitalization of, 74–75
    of direct address, 57
    plural of, 82
Nouns, types of
    collective, 20, 30–31
    count and noncount, 44–47
    generic, 30
    possessive, 63–64
    proper versus common,
      74–75
nowheres, 165
number, amount, 159–60
Number and person
    and agreement with verb,
      18–22
    shifts in, 7–8
Numbers mentioned as
    numbers
    italics for, 80
    plural of, 64–65
Numbers versus figures,
    78–79

Object complement, 172
Objective case
    personal pronouns, 33–35
    who, whom, 35–36
Objects
    direct, 170
    indirect, 171
    objective case for, 33–35
    of prepositions, 173
of, 165
off of, 165
Omissions, indicated by
    apostrophe, 64
    ellipsis mark, 72, 97
Omitted words, 6–7, 49–50
only, placement of, 10
or. See also Coordinating
    conjunctions
    subjects joined by, 19

Parallelism, 5–6
Paraphrases
    and avoiding plagiarism,
      94
    integrating, 99–100
Parentheses, 71
    no comma before, 59
Parenthetical citations
    APA style, 123–25
    MLA style, 103–07
Parenthetical elements
    commas with, 56
    dashes with, 70–71
Participial phrases, 172
Participles, past and present,
    172–73
Parts of speech, 173
passed, past, 165
Passive voice, 3–5, 28, 168
Past participles, 172
    of irregular verbs, 22–25
    of regular verbs, 22
Past perfect tense, 26
Past progressive form, 27
Past tense, 26
    and irregular verbs,
      22–25
    versus past perfect, 27
Percentages, figures for, 79
Perfect tenses, 26
    ESL problems with, 48
Period, 69
    with abbreviations, 69
    with ellipsis mark, 72
    with quotation marks, 66
Personal pronouns, 173
    case of, 33–35
Person, number
    shifts in, 7–8
    and subject–verb
      agreement, 18
Phrases, 173. *See also*
    Phrases, types of
    empty or inflated, 2–3
    fragmented, 39–40
    introductory, comma after,
      52–53
    misplaced, 10–11
    restrictive, nonrestrictive,
      54–55, 58
Phrases, types of
    absolute, 168
    appositive, 169
    gerund, 170
    infinitive, 171

Phrases, types of (*cont.*)
  participial, 172
  prepositional, 173
Plagiarism, 91–95
Plurals. *See also* Agreement
  of abbreviations, 64
  of letters used as letters, 64
  of numbers, 64–65
  spelling, 82
  of words used as words, 64
plus, 165
P.M., A.M., p.m., a.m., 77
Point of view, 7–8
Possessive case
  with apostrophe, 63–64
  with gerund, 35
Possessive nouns. *See*
  Possessive case
Possessive pronouns, 173
precede, proceed, 165
Predicate, 173
Predicate adjective. *See*
  Subject complement
Predicate noun. *See* Subject
  complement
Prefixes, hyphen after, 85
Prepositional phrases, 173
Prepositions, 173
Present participle, 173
  in participial phrases, 172
  and progressive forms, 27
Present perfect tense, 26
Present progressive form, 27
Present tense, 26, 27
  subject-verb agreement
  in, 18–22
principal, principle, 165
proceed, precede, 165
Progressive verb forms,
  26–27, 48
Pronoun-antecedent agree-
  ment, 29–31
Pronoun case
  I versus *me*, etc., 33–35
  possessive case, 35, 63–64
  who, whom, 35–36
Pronoun reference, 31–32
Pronouns, 174
  problems with, 28–36
Proper nouns
  capitalization of, 74–75
  the with, 45–47
*Publication Manual of the
  American Psychological
  Association*, 157

Punctuation, 51–72
  with quotation marks,
  66–69
  spacing with, 117–18, 132

Question mark, 69–70
  with quotation marks, 67
quotation, quote, 165
Quotation marks, 65–69. *See
  also* Quotations
Quotations. *See also* Quotation marks
  avoiding plagiarism, 92–95
  brackets with, 71–72,
  96–97
  capitalization in, 75–76
  citing, 92–93
  ellipsis marks with, 72,
  96–97
  integrating, 95–99
  long, 98
  punctuation of, 65–69
  within quotations, 65
  with signal phrase, 95–96
quote, quotation, 165

real, really, 165
reason is because, 166
reason why, 166
Redundancies, 2
Reference of pronouns,
  31–32
References
  APA style, 126–31, 136
  Chicago style (Bibliogra-
  phy), 144–49, 155
  MLA style (Works Cited),
  108–16, 121
Reflexive pronoun. *See* In-
  tensive pronoun
Regular verbs, 22, 174
Relative adverbs, 174
Relative pronouns, 174
  agreement with verb, 21
  ESL problems with, 50
  who, whom, 35–36
Repetition
  ESL problems with, 50
  unnecessary, 2
Researched writing, 86–101.
  See also Documenta-
  tion; Manuscript
  formats
  citing sources, 91–92
  facts and statistics in, 101

organization of evidence,
88–89
paraphrases and
summaries in, 99–100
plagiarism, avoiding,
92–95
quotations in, 95–99
supporting points, 90
thesis in, 87–88
respectfully, respectively, 166
Restrictive elements, no
commas with, 58
Run-on sentences, 41–44

-s
and apostrophe, 63–65
and spelling, 82
as verb ending, 18
Second-person point of
view, 7–8
self-, hyphen with, 85
Semicolon, 59–61
to correct run-on
sentence, 43
with quotation marks,
66–67
sensual, sensuous, 166
Sentence fragments, 39–41
Sentences, 174. *See also*
Sentence types
choppy, 12–13
fragments, 39–41
run-on, 41–44
thesis, 87–88
variety in, 12–14
wordy, 2–3
Sentence types
complex, 169
compound, 169
compound–complex,
169
simple, 174
Series
comma with, 53
parallelism and, 5
parentheses with, 71
semicolon with, 60
set, sit, 166
Sexist language, 16, 30
shall, as modal, 47–48
she versus *her*, 33–35
Shifts, 7–9
should, as modal, 47–48
should of, 166
sic, 72

Signal phrases
to introduce sources,
95–96, 98–101
in MLA citation, 103–07
Simple sentence, 174
Simple subject, 174
Simple tenses, 26
since, 166
sit, set, 166
site, cite, 161
Slang, 15
Slash, 72
so. See Coordinating
conjunctions
*somebody, someone,
something*, 19–20, 29–30
sort of, kind of, 164
Spelling, 81–84
Split infinitive, 12
Style manuals, list of, 156–57
Subject, grammatical, 174
after verb, 13–14, 20–21,
174
and agreement with verb,
18–22
case of, 33–35
ESL problems with,
49–50
of infinitive, 35
understood, 175
Subject complement, 174
adjective as, 33–34
case of, 33–34
Subjective case, 33–35
Subject-verb agreement,
18–22
Subjunctive mood, 28
Subordinate clauses, 175
fragmented, 39
minor ideas in, 12–13
Subordinating conjunctions,
175
Subordination, 12–13
Subtitles, 62, 75
such as
no colon after, 63
no comma after, 58
Suffixes, hyphen before, 85
Summaries
documenting, 91–92
integrating, 99–100
and plagiarism, 92–95
Superlative form of adjectives and adverbs, 38
suppose to, use to, 167

sure and, 166
Syllables, division of, 85

take, bring, 160–61
teach, learn, 164
Tenses, verb, 25–27
   and agreement with sub-
      ject, 18–22
   ESL problems with, 47–49
   shifts in, 8–9
than
   no comma before, 59
   parallelism with, 6
   pronoun after, 34–35
   omitted words with, 7
than, then, 166
that
   agreement of verb with,
      21
   omission of, 7
   versus *which,* 54–55, 166
   versus *who,* 167
the. See Articles
   ESL problems with, 44–47
their, there, they're, 166–67
theirselves, 166
them, nonstandard use of,
   166
them versus *they,* 33–35
then, than, 166
there. See there is, there are
there, their, they're, 166–67
therefore
   comma after, 56
   semicolon with, 56, 60
there is, there are
   ESL problems with, 49–50
   as expletive, 170
   and subject-verb
      agreement, 21
Thesis, 87–89
they
   indefinite reference of, 32
   nonstandard for *their,* 167
   versus *them,* 33–35
they're, their, there, 166–67
Third-person point of view,
   7–8
this, reference of, 31–32
Time
   abbreviations for, 77
   colon with, 62
   numbers in, 79
Title page
   APA paper, 131–32, 134

Chicago-style paper, 150,
   152
   MLA paper, 117, 119
Titles of persons
   abbreviations with names,
      76–77
   capitalization of, 75
   comma with, 58
Titles of works
   capitalization of, 75, 133
   italics for, 79–80
   quotation marks for, 66
   treated as singular, 22
to, too, two, 167
toward, towards, 167
Transitional phrases
   commas with, 56
   semicolon with, 60
Transitive verbs, 175
try and, 167
two, to, too, 167

Underlining, 79–81
Understood subject, 175
unique, 167
Usage, glossary of, 159–68
use to, suppose to, 167
us versus *we,* 33–35

Variety, in sentences, 12–14
Verbal phrases, 175
Verbs, 175. *See also* Verbs,
   types of
   agreement with subject,
      18–22
   ESL problems with,
      47–49
   mood of, 28
   omission of, 49–50
   -*s* form of, 18
   shifts in tense, 8–9
   tenses. *See* Tenses,
      verb
   voice of, 3–5, 28
Verbs, types of
   active versus passive, 3–5,
      28, 168
   helping and main, 47–49,
      170
   linking, 37–38, 171
   regular and irregular,
      22–25, 174
   transitive and intransitive,
      175
Voice, of verb

active versus passive, 3–5, 28, 168

wait for, wait on, 167
was versus *were,* 18–22
ways, 167
weather, whether, 167
well, good, 37, 163
were versus *was,* 18–22
we versus *us,* 33–35
where, 167
whether . . . or, 5–6
whether, weather, 167
which, agreement with verb, 21
which versus *that,* 54–55, 166
which versus *who,* 167
while, 167
who
agreement of verb with, 21
versus *which* or *that,* 167
versus *whom,* 35–36, 167
who's, whose, 168
will, as modal, 47–48
Word division, 85
Wordiness, 2–3

Words
compound, 84–85
division of, 85
foreign, italics for, 80
omitted, 6–7
Words as words
italics for, 80
plural of, 64
quotation marks for, 66
treated as singular, 22
Works cited
APA style (references), 126–31, 136
Chicago style (bibliography), 144–49, 155
MLA style, 108–16, 121
would, as modal, 47–48
would of, 168

yet. See Coordinating conjunctions
you
indefinite use of, 32, 168
as personal pronoun, 173
point of view, 7–8
your, you're, 168

Checklist for Global Revision

FOCUS

► Is the thesis stated clearly enough?
  Is it placed where readers will notice it?

► Does each idea support the thesis?

ORGANIZATION

► Can readers easily follow the structure?
  Would headings help?

► Do topic sentences signal new ideas?

► Are ideas presented in a logical order?

CONTENT

► Is the supporting material persuasive?

► Are important ideas fully developed?

► Is the draft concise enough — free of irrelevant
  or repetitious material?

► Are the parts proportioned sensibly?
  Do major ideas receive enough attention?

STYLE

► Is the voice appropriate — not too stuffy, not
  too breezy?

► Are the sentences clear, emphatic, and varied?

USE OF QUOTATIONS

► Is quoted material introduced with a signal
  phrase and documented with a citation?

► Is quoted material enclosed within quotation
  marks (unless it has been set off from the text)?

► Is each quotation word-for-word accurate?
  If not, do brackets or ellipsis dots mark the
  changes or omissions?

USE OF OTHER SOURCE MATERIAL

► Is the draft free of plagiarism? Are summaries
  and paraphrases written in the writer's own
  words — not copied or half-copied from the
  source?

► Has source material that is not common
  knowledge been documented?

Correction Symbols

abbr	faulty abbreviation **23a**	**:**	colon **18b**
ad	adverb or adjective **13**	**؛**	apostrophe **19**
add	add needed word **4**	**" "**	quotation marks **20**
agr	agreement **10, 12a**	**.**	period **21a**
appr	inappropriate language **9**	**?**	question mark **21b**
art	article **16a**	**!**	exclamation point **21c**
awk	awkward	**—**	dash **21d**
cap	capital letter **22**	**( )**	parentheses **21e**
case	case **12c, 12d**	**[ ]**	brackets **21f**
cs	comma splice **15**	**. . .**	ellipsis mark **21g**
dm	dangling modifier **7c**	**/**	slash **21h**
-ed	*-ed* ending **11a**	*pass*	ineffective passive **2, 11d**
emph	emphasis **2**	*ref*	pronoun reference **12b**
ESL	English as a second language **16**	*run-on*	run-on sentence **15**
frag	sentence fragment **14**	*-s*	*-s* ending on verb **10, 16b**
fs	fused sentence **15**	*sexist*	sexist language **9c, 12a**
hyph	hyphen **24b**	*shift*	confusing shift **5**
irreg	irregular verb **11a**	*sl*	slang **9b**
ital	italics (underlining) **23c**	*sp*	misspelled word **24a**
jarg	jargon **9a**	*s-v*	subject-verb agreement **10**
lc	use lowercase letter **22**	*t*	verb tense **11b**
mix	mixed construction **6**	*usage*	see Glossary of Usage
mm	misplaced modifier **7a–b, 7d**	*v*	voice **2, 11d**
mood	mood **11c**	*var*	sentence variety **8**
num	numbers **23b**	*vb*	problem with verb **11, 16b–c**
om	omitted word **4, 16a, 16c**	*w*	wordy **1**
p	punctuation	*//*	faulty parallelism **3**
؛	comma **17a–i**	**^**	insert
no ,	no comma **17j**	**x**	obvious error
;	semicolon **18a**	**#**	insert space
		⌒	close up space

Contents

CLARITY | 1

1. Wordy sentences | 2
a. Redundancies
b. Empty or inflated phrases
c. Complex structures
2. Active verbs | 3
a. versus *be* verbs
b. versus passive verbs
3. Parallelism | 5
a. Items in a series
b. Paired ideas
4. Needed words | 6
a. In compound structures
b. *That*
c. In comparisons
5. Shifts | 7
a. Point of view
b. Tense
6. Mixed constructions | 9
a. Mixed grammar
b. Illogical connections
7. Misplaced and dangling modifiers | 10
a. Misplaced words
b. Misplaced phrases and clauses
c. Dangling modifiers
d. Split infinitives
8. Sentence variety | 12
a. Choppy sentences
b. Sentence openings
9. Appropriate voice | 14
a. Jargon
b. Slang
c. Sexist language

GRAMMAR | 17

10. Subject-verb agreement | 18
a. Words between subject and verb
b. Subjects with *and*
c. Subjects with *or, nor*
d. Indefinite pronouns such as *someone*
e. Collective nouns such as *jury*
f. Subject after verb
g. *Who, which, that*
h. Plural form, singular meaning
i. Titles and words as words
11. Other problems with verbs | 22
a. Irregular verbs
b. Tense
c. Mood
d. Voice
12. Problems with pronouns | 28
a. Agreement
b. Reference
c. Case of personal pronouns such as *I* versus *me*
d. *Who* or *whom*
13. Adjectives and adverbs | 36
a. Adverbs
b. Adjectives
c. Comparatives and superlatives
14. Sentence fragments | 39
a. Clauses
b. Phrases
c. Acceptable fragments
15. Run-on sentences | 41
a. Revision with comma and coordinating conjunction
b. With semicolon
c. By separating sentences
d. By restructuring the sentence
16. ESL problems | 44
a. Articles
b. Helping verbs and main verbs
c. Omitted subjects, expletives, verbs
d. Repeated subjects, objects

PUNCTUATION | 51

17. The comma | 52
a. Independent clauses with coordinating conjunction
b. Introductory elements
c. Items in a series
d. Coordinate adjectives
e. Nonrestrictive elements
f. Transitions, absolute phrases, contrasts
g. Direct address, *yes* and *no*, interrogative tags, interjections
h. *He said,* etc.
i. Dates, addresses, titles
j. Misuses
18. The semicolon and the colon | 59
a. The semicolon